NEW DIRECTIONS FOR COMMUNITY COLLEGES

Arthur M. Cohen   Florence B. Brawer
EDITOR-IN-CHIEF   ASSOCIATE EDITOR

R. Dean Gerdeman
PUBLICATION COORDINATOR

The Community College Role in Welfare to Work

C. David Lisman
University of Denver

EDITOR

Number 116, Winter 2001

 JOSSEY-BASS
A Wiley Company
www.josseybass.com

378.154
C.T

ERIC®
Clearinghouse for Community Colleges

THE COMMUNITY COLLEGE ROLE IN WELFARE TO WORK
C. David Lisman (ed.)
New Directions for Community Colleges, no. 116
Arthur M. Cohen, Editor-in-Chief
Florence B. Brawer, Associate Editor

New Directions for Community Colleges is indexed in Current Index to Journals in Education (ERIC).

Microfilm copies of issues and articles are available in 16mm and 35mm, as well as microfiche in 105mm, through University Microfilms Inc., 300 North Zeeb Road, Ann Arbor, Michigan 48106-1346.

ISSN 0194-3081   electronic ISSN 1536-0733   ISBN 0-7879-5781-X

NEW DIRECTIONS FOR COMMUNITY COLLEGES is part of The Jossey-Bass Higher and Adult Education Series and is published quarterly by Jossey-Bass, 989 Market Street, San Francisco, California 94103-1741, in association with the ERIC Clearinghouse for Community Colleges. Periodicals postage paid at San Francisco, California, and at additional mailing offices. POSTMASTER: Send address changes to New Directions for Community Colleges, Jossey-Bass, 989 Market Street, San Francisco, California 94103-1741.

SUBSCRIPTIONS cost $66.00 for individuals and $135.00 for institutions, agencies, and libraries. Prices subject to change.

THE MATERIAL in this publication is based on work sponsored wholly or in part by the Office of Educational Research and Improvement, U.S. Department of Education, under contract number ED-99-CO-0010. Its contents do not necessarily reflect the views of the Department or any other agency of the U.S. Government.

EDITORIAL CORRESPONDENCE should be sent to the Editor-in-Chief, Arthur M. Cohen, at the ERIC Clearinghouse for Community Colleges, University of California, 3051 Moore Hall, Box 951521, Los Angeles, California 90095-1521. All manuscripts receive anonymous reviews by external referees.

Cover photograph © Rene Sheret, After Image, Los Angeles, California, 1990.

Printed in the United States of America on acid-free recycled paper containing 100 percent recovered waste paper, of which at least 20 percent is postconsumer waste.

CONTENTS

Editor's Notes

On August 23, 1996, President Clinton signed the Personal Responsibility and Work Opportunity Reconciliation Act (PRWORA), which replaced the Aid to Families with Dependent Children (AFDC) welfare program. Under the new legislation, a new block grant, Temporary Assistance for Needy Families (TANF), was launched in July 1997, eliminating welfare entitlements. Under AFDC, single parents with dependent children could qualify for welfare assistance for as long as they had dependent children. Under the TANF program, welfare recipients have a five-year lifetime limit of welfare assistance. Within the five-year limit, single parents with dependent children can qualify for welfare assistance for only two years at a time. At the end of two years, welfare recipients must be involved in some form of federally or state-approved work activities.

One of the important changes of welfare reform is that each state has the authority to decide how to implement the TANF program, following federal guidelines. In fact, states have been allowed to pass this authority on to counties through their county commissioners. The decentralization of TANF has created many opportunities and challenges for the implementation of the program.

Two challenges that community colleges have faced are the work-first philosophy of many TANF programs and the problems of dealing with multiple constituencies in developing training programs. Many states have elected to require able-bodied individuals to get a job immediately rather than allowing them to receive some form of short-term job training to make them more employable. This policy illustrates a belief that the dependent nature of the system rather than the effects of poverty is the greatest contributor to people being on welfare. In line with this thinking, many states, including Oregon, Wisconsin, and Florida, have essentially mandated that welfare recipients get a job and leave the welfare system. Community colleges have found it necessary to make a variety of adjustments to meet the requirements of these types of programs. Some have developed community service programs to provide nonpaid work experiences to enable individuals to continue to qualify for welfare benefits. Others have developed an increasing number of fast-track training programs to accommodate the work-first philosophy, which prohibits welfare recipients from studying for an associate degree.

Under AFDC programs, the city and county social service agencies supervised this program, whereas many different agencies have implemented TANF programs, depending on the states. In some cases, the county social service agencies have continued to manage the program. Even then, social service agencies have divested themselves of some traditional features of case management, such as requiring training vendors to provide case managers. The overall challenge has been for community colleges to develop comprehensive and well-designed programs that satisfy the needs of the agencies that are implementing welfare reform. It has been difficult for some colleges to become involved in a collaborative process of developing a coherent training program that matches the TANF program needs because they have found that they have had to compete with other training vendors for clients.

Because of the urgent situation of many welfare recipients, it has been difficult for community colleges to take a more comprehensive look at the problems of poverty and become involved with communities to address many of the underlying problems, such as a lack of well-paying jobs, affordable housing, and adequate child care. A related federal initiative, the Workforce Investment Act (WIA), has also presented opportunities and challenges for community colleges in serving this population. The WIA is restructuring the funding streams to provide a generic funding base for individuals who qualify for job training support through job training centers. WIA also has brought about the restructuring of one-stop job training centers. Under federal law, the one-stop centers are allowed to provide job search and job search skill training in-house. Other job training is supposed to be outsourced to vendors, such as community colleges. These changes are creating some of the same vendor challenges to community colleges as the TANF initiative. However, these different funding streams provide significant opportunities for entrepreneurial colleges to develop pre- and post-training programs involving certificates and even using Pell grants.

This issue provides a candid assessment of the policy issues related to welfare reform and provides examples of best practices of how to progress in the future with respect to this issue. The policy issue chapters (Chapters One through Four) assess the impact of welfare reform and the local and statewide matters that must be considered in developing effective welfare-to-work programs. In the best-practice chapters (Chapters Five through Nine), each contributor provides practical examples of training programs that work and analyzes the challenges and opportunities that welfare reform has presented to them as they have developed and implemented these programs.

Policy Issues

Chapter One, by Thomas Brock, Lisa Matus-Grossman, and Gayle Hamilton, examines the opportunities and challenges for community colleges presented by TANF. The chapter draws on research conducted by the Manpower Demonstration Research Corporation, a nonprofit, nonpartisan research organization that has evaluated the implementation and effects of welfare-to-work programs across the United States.

Successful participation in welfare to work requires that college leaders integrate welfare to work into the college mission, provide support for

staff participating in the programs, and build consensus with external partners. In Chapter Two, Pamila J. Fisher discusses the policy and programmatic issues that Modesto Junior College faced in implementing its TANF
program. Fisher describes the creation of a countywide welfare reform steering committee and the college's coordinated efforts to ensure smooth implementation of a comprehensive welfare-to-work program.

In Chapter Three, Kathleen Vespa Pampe discusses community colleges
and welfare to work from a rural perspective, the barriers to rural welfare
recipients in terms of job placement, and the necessity of collaborative
efforts and partnerships for successful welfare-to-work programs. The chapter examines some of welfare policies in Illinois relative to education and
training and the overall picture of rural welfare reform efforts.

Wisconsin was a leader in implementing welfare reform based on the
work-first model. In Chapter Four, Dennis Nitschke documents experiences
in implementing a work-first approach at a technical college in Wisconsin.
The redesign of the college's curriculum for short-term training, the role of
the business and social services staff in this training, and the accountability
measures applied were positive learning experiences for the college. However, the eventual elimination of training from the final state welfare law and
the perceived emphasis on measuring how quickly individuals can be
removed from the welfare rolls proved to be shortsighted.

Best Practices

In Chapter Five, Karen Pagenette and Cheryl Kozell describe the Advanced
Technology Program at Oakland Community College in Michigan, the 1998
winner of the American Association of Community Colleges competition
for exemplary welfare-to-work training programs. With $100,000 in pilot
funding, the college developed a community-based task force and formed
partnerships with local corporations to provide an advanced technology-
training program for the welfare population. This chapter describes the
operation of the program, the nature of the business and community partnerships, and the benefits and challenges of replicating the program at other
community colleges.

Chapter Six, by John W. Ream, Brenda G. Wagner, and Robin C. Knorr,
describes the development and implementation of a successful program at
Metropolitan Community College in Missouri to train welfare recipients for
jobs in call center customer service departments. In Chapter Seven, Daniela
Higgins highlights the importance of postsecondary education to help people stay employed and move up the economic ladder and provides a description of welfare programs and services at Colorado's Community College of
Aurora Center for Workforce Development.

Arguing that the welfare reform model actually tracks families, especially
single parent and minority families, into long-term poverty, Kathleen Bombach discusses in Chapter Eight a new model for welfare to work developed

in El Paso, Texas. This program offers a fully articulated pathway from literacy and basic job skills training into associate and bachelor's degree programs designed to result in long-term family economic self-sufficiency.

In Chapter Nine, Patricia C. Higgins, Janice Mayne, Patricia Deacon, and Elena LaComb discuss the JOBSplus! program at Onondaga Community College in New York. The chapter provides examples of practices designed to meet the special needs of welfare recipients and lead to job readiness, retention, and satisfaction. In Chapter Ten, Katalin Szelènyi highlights ERIC documents that present studies, initiatives, and trends related to the welfare student population and welfare-to-work programs at community colleges.

C. David Lisman
Editor

C. DAVID LISMAN is director of the Center for Service Learning and Civic Engagement at the University of Denver. Formerly he was a philosophy professor and director of the Center for Community and Workforce Development at the Community College of Aurora, where he established their welfare-to-work program.

1

This chapter presents the results of a national study examining the effectiveness of employment- and education-focused welfare-to-work programs and considers the implications for community colleges.

Welfare Reform and Community Colleges: A Policy and Research Context

Thomas Brock, Lisa Matus-Grossman, Gayle Hamilton

For almost as long as there has been welfare, there have been efforts at reform, but none has been as dramatic as the Personal Responsibility and Work Opportunity Reconciliation Act (PRWORA), passed by Congress in 1996. PRWORA replaced the nation's primary cash assistance program, Aid to Families with Dependent Children (AFDC), with Temporary Assistance for Needy Families (TANF). As a result, welfare recipients can no longer collect benefits indefinitely and are under strong pressure to find work. Community colleges, which have long been players in helping welfare recipients and other low-income people acquire skills and gain entry or advance in the labor force, face new opportunities and challenges in delivering education, training, and other services to the welfare population.

For over twenty-five years, the Manpower Demonstration Research Corporation (MDRC), a nonprofit, nonpartisan research organization, has studied the implementation and effects of programs that have attempted to increase self-sufficiency and improve the life circumstances of people on welfare. In this chapter, we review some major findings and consider their implications for community colleges. We focus in particular on recent findings from the National Evaluation of Welfare-to-Work Strategies (NEWWS), a federally initiated study that answers two key questions asked by those who run welfare-to-work programs: What works best? and for whom? We also draw on the early findings from Opening Doors to Earning Credentials, a foundation-sponsored initiative that is examining ways to eliminate barriers and expand opportunities for welfare recipients and low-wage workers in postsecondary education.

Evidence on Welfare-to-Work Programs from the NEWWS Evaluation

The work-first emphasis of PRWORA raises an important question for welfare policymakers, administrators, and service providers: What is the best way to move people into employment?[1] In the 1980s, many states opted to run mandatory job search programs, in which welfare recipients were taught how to look for work and were provided with job leads (U.S. General Accounting Office, 1987). Rigorous research on these programs found that they speeded up the entry of welfare recipients into the labor market but did not lead to jobs that were long lasting or high paying. Furthermore, the programs generally did not benefit the most disadvantaged welfare recipients (Gueron and Pauly, 1991; Friedlander and Burtless, 1995). Many policymakers and program operators wondered whether an upfront investment in basic education and skill development would lead to better results than the labor force attachment (LFA), or job search, approach. Proponents of this alternative approach argued that human capital development (HCD) programs, focused on the development of basic skills through education, would help people get better and more stable jobs and reduce returns to welfare rolls.

The NEWWS Evaluation was launched in 1989 to settle this debate and answer other questions about the implementation, effects, and costs of welfare-to-work programs. Conceived and funded by the U.S. Department of Health and Human Services, with support from the U.S. Department of Education, the evaluation was conducted in seven locations across the United States: Atlanta, Georgia; Grand Rapids, Michigan; Riverside, California; Columbus, Ohio; Detroit, Michigan; Oklahoma City, Oklahoma; and Portland, Oregon. In each of these locations, or sites, employment- or education-focused programs were operated over several years.

Individuals who were mandated to participate in welfare-to-work programs—predominantly single mothers with children age three and above (or, in some sites, age one and above) (U.S. House of Representatives, 1993)—were randomly assigned to program or control groups. Program group members were required to participate in welfare-to-work activities or risk a financial sanction, usually resulting in the removal of the adult from the cash grant. Control group members were neither required nor allowed to participate in welfare-to-work programs and could not be sanctioned; they could, however, enroll in other services available in the community if they wished. The strength of this design is that it ensures that the characteristics of program and control group members at the time of entering the study—their education levels, work histories, family circumstances, motivation, and so forth—are statistically the same. Consequently, any subsequent differences in the two groups' outcomes can be attributed to the welfare-to-work programs.

As part of a largely unprecedented effort to determine which of the two different welfare-to-work strategies was more effective, three of the sites in the NEWWS evaluation—Atlanta, Grand Rapids, and Riverside—agreed to operate two distinct welfare-to-work programs simultaneously: an LFA program and an HCD program. Each communicated a different message to welfare recipients about the best route to employment and differed from the other in the way services were emphasized and sequenced. Random assignment was used to assign welfare recipients to the LFA or HCD programs or to a control group. This three-group design provides the strongest possible test of the LFA and HCD approaches by allowing a direct comparison of the LFA and HCD groups to the control group, or the LFA and HCD groups to each other.

Table 1.1 provides an overview of the programs and research designs for the seven sites. Atlanta, Grand Rapids, and Riverside were the only sites that ran LFA and HCD programs side by side. Columbus, Detroit, and Oklahoma City ran education-focused programs (similar to HCD), and Portland adopted a mixed approach. As was true nationally during the 1990s, the sites experienced employment growth and a falling unemployment rate between 1991 and 1999 and large declines in their welfare caseloads during the study period.

Sample Characteristics. Across the seven sites, sample intake took place from mid-1991 through the end of 1994 and resulted in over forty thousand welfare recipients randomly assigned to program and control groups. The typical sample member was female, about thirty years old, and either never married or separated, divorced, or widowed. In contrast to some stereotypes, the majority of sample members in five of the seven sites had at least six months of work experience with the same employer. Most, however, had not worked in the twelve months prior to random assignment. With regard to past welfare receipt, the majority in all sites but Oklahoma City had already received welfare for at least two years. Between 48 and 56 percent of sample members had a high school diploma or general educational development (GED) when they entered the program, and some enrollees in all sites had some college or postsecondary schooling. On average, however, sample members had completed only eleven years of schooling prior to random assignment. There was wide variation in the percentage of sample members who had enrolled in any education or training program in the twelve months before entering the study, ranging from a high of almost 40 percent in Grand Rapids (where community colleges, adult schools, and vocational training providers aggressively recruited welfare recipients) to just under 10 percent in Columbus. Most often, sample members who had enrolled in an activity chose a vocational education or skills training program.

Program Emphases. The LFA programs in Atlanta, Grand Rapids, and Riverside emphasized rapid employment and required job search as

Table 1.1. Programs and Research Designs for the Evaluation Sites

Characteristic	Atlanta	Grand Rapids	Riverside	Columbus	Detroit	Oklahoma City	Portland
Program types	LFA and HCD	LFA and HCD	LFA and HCD	Education focused	Education focused	Education focused	Employment and education blend
Sample size (total)	4,433	4,554	8,322	7,242	4,459	8,677	4,028
Program	1,441 (LFA) 1,495 (HCD)	1,557 (LFA) 1,542 (HCD)	3,384 (LFA) 1,596 (HCD)	2,513 (integrated) 2,570 (traditional)	2,226	4,309	3,529
Control	1,497	1,455	3,342	2,159	2,233	4,368	499

the first activity. Clients were instructed on how to look for work, complete a job application, and conduct an interview. Clients were generally instructed to take any job offer, including minimum-wage jobs, on the theory that they could best advance up the career ladder by building skills at the workplace. If clients did not succeed in finding employment through job search, they were assigned to education, vocational training, or work experience activities to improve their employability. LFA programs emphasized short-term assignments so that clients could return quickly to job search.

In contrast to the LFA approach, the HCD programs in Atlanta, Grand Rapids, and Riverside emphasized increasing skills through formal education and training before entering the labor market. The education-focused programs in Columbus, Detroit, and Oklahoma City shared this emphasis. Columbus also featured a traditional approach, in which separate staff members performed income maintenance and welfare-to-work case management roles, and an integrated approach, in which these functions were consolidated. Clients received an initial assessment to determine their work history, educational skills, and employment interests, followed by an assignment to an appropriate activity. Because of the generally low educational attainment of most welfare recipients, basic education (that is, adult basic education, GED, or English as a Second Language) was a common first step. College and vocational training programs, however, were encouraged for those who qualified. Job search was assigned after education or training was completed. By increasing clients' basic skills, HCD programs hoped to place clients in jobs that offered good pay, benefits, and stability of employment.

Portland was unique in that its program blended LFA and HCD elements. Like the LFA programs, Portland staff emphasized that employment was the goal of program participation. Clients who were considered job ready were assigned to job search for their first activity, but clients who were more disadvantaged, including those with low basic skills and little work history, were enrolled in education or training first, followed by job search. Portland employed full-time job developers to work with participants once they began looking for a job. In contrast to the pure LFA programs in the evaluation, Portland staff advised clients to be selective in their job search, accepting only positions that paid above minimum wage and provided benefits.

All of the evaluation sites used a brokered model of service delivery. Welfare department staff usually provided assessment and case management services and in most sites managed the job search and work experience components. Community colleges, adult schools, and vocational training centers provided basic education and occupational skills training courses (Hamilton and Brock, 1994). Portland was unusual in that the welfare department contracted with the community colleges to provide all of the key services (although case management responsibilities were shared with welfare staff).

In no other site did community colleges play such a central role.

Findings on Program Implementation and Participation. All of the NEWWS Evaluation sites produced significant increases in employment-related activities (including job search, education, or training) among program group members. (Recall that control group members could voluntarily participate in services other than those provided by the welfare-to-work programs.) Most of the programs achieved a participation impact (the difference between the participation levels of program and control group members) of 21 percentage points or more in the two years following individuals' entry into the study. The impacts ranged from 9 percent in Detroit to 40 percent in the Riverside HCD group. Among people who participated, involvement in employment-related activities usually lasted for at least several months (Freedman and others, 2000).

As displayed in Figure 1.1, the programs generally succeeded in increasing participation in the specific activities they tried to promote. For example, the LFA programs in Atlanta, Grand Rapids, and Riverside, along with Portland, achieved significant impacts in job search activities. The HCD programs in Atlanta, Grand Rapids, and Riverside, together with the education-focused programs in Columbus, achieved significant impacts in education or training. In Oklahoma City and Detroit, the differences between program and control group participation rates in education and training were much smaller (and not statistically significant in Detroit). The small participation impacts in Oklahoma City and Detroit were attributed to low enforcement of participation requirements for the program group (Freedman and others, 2000).

Longer-term data on participation are available for the LFA and HCD programs in Atlanta, Grand Rapids, and Riverside and for Portland. Even at five years after random assignment, the programs in these sites maintained statistically significant differences between program and control group members in employment activity participation levels, ranging from 9 percent in Portland to 27 percent in the Riverside HCD program. All of the programs had a substantial effect on job search participation. In addition, significant education or training impacts were found in the Atlanta LFA and HCD programs, Grand Rapids HCD program, Riverside HCD program, and Portland.

Individuals who entered the Atlanta, Grand Rapids, and Riverside HCD programs without a high school diploma or GED were more likely than control group members to obtain such a diploma during the follow-up period, a result consistent with program goals and not found in the LFA programs. In Portland, such nongraduates were more likely to obtain a trade license or certificate or to obtain a GED and then a second education or training credential. For those who entered the study with a high school diploma or GED, only the Atlanta programs—both LFA and HCD—led to significant positive effects on receiving any type of education or training credential.

Figure 1.1. Participation in Job Search by Promoted Activities

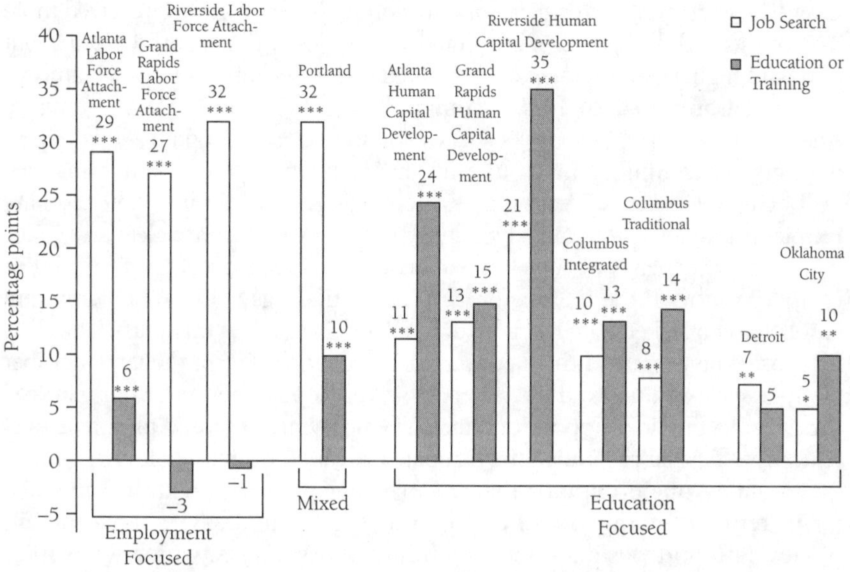

Percentage points

□ Job Search

▨ Education or Training

Riverside Labor Force Attachment

Atlanta Labor Force Attachment
29 ***

Grand Rapids Labor Force Attachment
27 ***
6 ***

32 ***
−3

Portland
32 ***
−1

Riverside Human Capital Development

Atlanta Human Capital Development
11 ***
24 ***

Grand Rapids Human Capital Development
35 ***
21 ***

Columbus Integrated
10 ***
13 ***

Columbus Traditional
13 ***
15 ***

Oklahoma City

Detroit
7 **
5 *

14 ***
8 ***
5

10 **
10 ***

40
35
30
25
20
15
10
5
0
−5

Employment Focused

Mixed

Education Focused

Program Effects on Employment, Earnings, Welfare, and Income.

Most control group members found employment on their own during the follow-up period. Nevertheless, the employment rates of program group members in the majority of sites were higher than the rate of the control group. For example, in the Riverside LFA program, 74.5 percent of the program group was employed over five years compared to 66.1 percent of the control group, for a difference (or impact) of 8.4 percent. Across the sites, significant employment impacts ranged from 1.9 to 8.4 percent. Most of the programs also increased enrollees' earnings over control group earnings during the follow-up period. Of the programs that produced significant earnings gains, the average increases ranged from $1,361 in the Riverside HCD program to $5,150 in Portland.

As with employment, most control group members succeeded in getting off welfare on their own during the follow-up period, but in the sites for which we have data, program group members moved off welfare sooner. The impacts ranged from an average reduction of 1.6 months on welfare in Detroit to an average reduction of 5.6 months in Portland. In dollar terms, program group members received between $710 and $2,949 less in welfare over five years than did their control group counterparts. The largest welfare savings occurred in the Riverside programs, due in part to California's relatively large welfare grant (resulting in bigger savings when people go off welfare than in states where grants are smaller).

Across all sites, the programs had little effect on income, that is, the combination of earnings, tax payments and credits, and public assistance benefits. Over five years, welfare recipients in most of the program groups received more in earnings and the earned income credit than those in the control groups, but also paid higher payroll taxes and received less in welfare and Food Stamps.

LFA Compared to HCD. Comparing the LFA and HCD programs in Atlanta, Grand Rapids, and Riverside, we found that HCD programs did not produce greater earnings gains or improvements in participants' overall financial well-being relative to LFA programs. Moreover, the LFA approach got welfare recipients into jobs more quickly than did the HCD approach, a clear advantage when welfare benefits are time limited. Finally, the LFA approach was much less costly to run than the HCD approach. These findings held true for program enrollees who lacked a high school diploma or GED as of study entry, as well as for those who possessed these educational credentials. Given the large number of programs examined and the variety of served populations and labor markets, these results provide support for choosing employment-focused programs over education-focused programs that mandate education or training for everyone.

Notably, one program—that in Portland—outperformed the others by far in terms of employment and earnings gains and saving government money. Portland was distinguished from the other sites, which were operating pure LFA or HCD programs, in that it initially assigned some enrollees to very short-term education or training and others (the majority) to job search. Portland staff also counseled participants to wait for a good job as opposed to taking the first job offered. This result, along with other research, suggests that a mixed approach that blends both employment search and education or training might be the most effective (see also Gueron and Pauly, 1991; Friedlander and Burtless, 1995).

The NEWWS results should not be interpreted as an indictment of the benefits of education and training in general. Additional analyses performed as part of this evaluation have suggested that obtaining a GED and, especially, obtaining a GED and then receiving some type of vocational training can result in employment and earnings gains for those who achieve these milestones. Using nonexperimental techniques, researchers estimated that those who received a GED earned $797 more on average than those who did not receive a GED over a three-year period. More impressive, those who earned a GED and received postsecondary services earned $1,542 more on average than those who did not (Bos, Scrivener, Snipes, and Hamilton, 2001).

Unfortunately, few NEWWS sample members made it this far. Although the Atlanta, Grand Rapids, and Riverside HCD programs increased GED certificate attainment by 7 to 11 percent for those who entered the study without a high school diploma or GED, only 10 to 23 percent of all HCD sample members who lacked these credentials at study entry had obtained one by the end of the five-year follow-up period. This suggests the need to identify other types of programs or initiatives that can achieve the originally hoped-for HCD goals of providing welfare recipients with better and more stable jobs and increasing their income.

Programmatic Implications for Community Colleges

In many ways, the analyses of PRWORA and the NEWWS data point to the same conclusion: welfare-to-work programs should have a strong employment emphasis. As evidenced in Portland, however, an employment-focused program can include education and training for people who need these services and can help clients obtain well-paying, stable jobs. Moreover, an employment-focused program can continue serving clients after they begin working, to help them acquire skills and earn credentials that will move them up the career ladder. In this section, we consider the variety of steps community colleges can take to accomplish these goals.

The first consideration for community colleges or any other organization designing a welfare-to-work program is to coordinate with local welfare agencies. Some colleges and welfare agencies enter into formal relationships, with a contract or memorandum of understanding that spells out the services that each institution will provide, the number of clients to be served, and the funding. Other colleges operate programs independent of the welfare system, with no explicit agreement to accept referrals or resources from the welfare department. In either case, they need to be aware of the local welfare agency's policies concerning education, training, and work activities. Otherwise, welfare recipients who enroll in community college programs may be at risk of being pulled out by welfare department case managers and placed in other activities or, worse, sanctioned because their activities do not count toward the welfare agency's participation requirement.

Running an employment-focused program does not mean that community colleges need to limit their offerings to job search or other work activities. As Portland demonstrated, job search can be used for job-ready clients, and short-term education and training can be used for clients in need of skills. Another approach is to combine education and training activities with work. Many welfare agencies currently allow welfare recipients to participate in ten or more hours of education or training per week provided that they work at least twenty hours. Some community colleges have developed work-study options to help welfare recipients meet their work obligations while going to school. Ideally, work-study positions can be structured to reinforce clients' career goals through placements in the college's administrative offices, student services, library, other facilities, or even off-campus with local public or nonprofit employers. At least two states, California and Kentucky, have created special work-study programs for TANF recipients that allow placements in off-campus for-profit employers, to provide participants with relevant career experience.

Although welfare-to-work programs will likely be relatively short term compared to a college's degree or certificate programs, it may be possible to condense programs into shorter time frames without sacrificing quality by increasing their intensity or combining different elements. For example, basic skills remediation and job training can be integrated rather than addressed separately (Grubb, Badway, Bell, and Castellano, 1999). Another option is to pair employment services with longer education and training programs that have been broken down into smaller modules that build on one another. In this way, recipients can earn credits or build skills in shorter, more manageable chunks. Participants who leave early do not need to repeat entire semester-long courses but can complete the remaining modules later (Golonka and Matus-Grossman, 2001). Still another option, often combined with modularizing programs, is to run programs in an open entry–open exit format, so that participants can move at their own pace and have the option of reenrolling if employment or other circumstances cause them to leave the program.

These various strategies suggest that welfare-to-work programs may be only the first step in a longer-term process of career development. Given the pressures and incentives for welfare recipients to find work, it may not be realistic to expect them to earn degrees or certificates in the short term. The challenge for community colleges is to leave open the door so that former welfare recipients return to gain such credentials in the future.

The Opening Doors Initiative

In 2001, MDRC launched the Opening Doors to Earning Credentials project to explore the issues of community college access and retention for current and former welfare recipients and low-wage workers.[2] The project is examining the full range of programs that community colleges can offer and how welfare recipients and low-wage workers might take better advantage of them. The encouraging early findings suggest that much can be done under existing state or federal welfare policies.

Balancing Work and School. In the past, community colleges and other welfare-to-work service providers could assume that most welfare recipients who enrolled in their programs were unemployed. Now, because of PRWORA's work requirements and the earned-income disregards adopted by many states, many welfare recipients are working at least part time. This suggests that community college programs should be designed to allow work and academic or training activities to be combined easily.

There is a huge variation across states and even localities in terms of the sorts of activities that are allowed to count toward the federal work requirement. Some states and localities insist on twenty or thirty hours of work per week in either paid employment or unpaid work experience. Other states have allowed welfare recipients to count some postsecondary participation toward the work requirement while still requiring some limited work hours. A growing number of states allow welfare recipients to engage in postsecondary or vocational education activities for one, two, or even four years without requiring additional work hours (Greenberg, Strawn, and Plimpton, 2000). Illinois has gone so far as to stop the clock for welfare recipients enrolled in full-time postsecondary degree-granting programs, meaning that they do not lose months under the time limit while they are in college.

Welfare recipients who are working and attending college often experience conflicts between employer and classroom demands because of dynamic or inflexible schedules, the need to put in overtime, or other issues. Colleges in some states provide on- or off-site work-study or internship positions to help participants fulfill their work requirement. Other colleges have hired job developers or placement staff to help welfare recipients find part-time private sector employment that will easily accommodate their school schedules. Ideally, such positions can provide entry into organizations or occupational fields that correspond to participants' career interests.

Family Demands and Responsibilities. By definition, all welfare recipients are also parents and will likely have competing family responsibilities in addition to any program or employer commitments. In a study of young mothers on welfare, Quint, Musick, and Ladner (1994) found that juggling family, school, and sometimes work, as well as pregnancy, were all barriers to finishing college degree or certificate programs. The more a community college program can take into account this delicate balancing act, the greater is the likelihood that working parents will be able to participate. Programs may wish to consider including children or other family members in program activities, with their parents or in separate enrichment programs, to ease child care problems and encourage greater levels of participation. Programs can also schedule activities on a flexible basis, as Riverside Community College's New Visions program has done by offering multiple sessions of a single activity so that parents with changing work schedules or child care arrangements can switch back and forth from an evening class to a daytime or weekend offering when necessary (Fein, Beecroft, Long, and Catalfamo, 2000).

Academic Barriers. The target population for welfare-to-work programs is relatively heterogeneous, with a variety of basic skill levels. In all but one NEWWS Evaluation site, at least 40 percent of welfare-to-work program enrollees did not have a high school diploma or GED. Nevertheless, many NEWWS enrollees had completed high school or a GED program before entering the study, and a small number had received some college or training. Another study estimated that welfare recipients fell almost evenly across three skill levels: 31 percent of recipients had "minimal" skills (the equivalent of having dropped out of high school), 3 percent had "basic" skills (the equivalent of having earned a high school diploma with below-average school performance), and 3 percent had "competent, advanced or superior" skills (the equivalent of some postsecondary education, a bachelor's degree, or beyond) (Carnevale and Desrochers, 1999, p. 6).

For program designers, these data suggest the importance of upfront screening or assessment to determine whether welfare recipients are ready for postsecondary-level course work or will require remediation and an individualized service delivery approach. Many community colleges are equipped to provide a full range of educational services; if they are not, they should be prepared to refer clients to other services in the community.

Personal Barriers. Participants may exhibit a variety of personal participation barriers, including poor physical health, depression, mental illness, substance abuse, or domestic violence. Some participants may have legal barriers to employment, such as past criminal records or unresolved immigration issues. In order to address such barriers, colleges may need to develop or provide referrals to counseling services that go beyond traditional academic counseling. This is another area where it makes sense for community college and welfare staff to coordinate, because welfare agencies often have contracts or linkages with programs that can help individuals with severe problems.

To help welfare recipients cope with more common concerns, such as the stress associated with reentering school or balancing home, school, and work commitments, some colleges have encouraged the formation of peer support networks. Welfare recipients come together on a regular basis, sometimes with college staff present, to discuss problems, seek advice, and gain emotional support. Sacramento City College in California, for example, has trained current TANF students to provide referrals through the Student Ambassador program to college and community resources as well as emotional support to students in need. The students involved in the program are paid for providing counseling and support as part of their work-study assignment.

Financial Cost. Welfare recipients who are interested in enrolling in associate degree programs or other community college courses may be deterred by the registration fees and other expenses related to school. Despite the availability of grants and loans, many welfare recipients may not be aware of how to apply for financial aid or feel intimidated by the process. Quint, Musick, and Ladner (1994) identified lack of understanding of financial aid or other college rules as a reason some young mothers on welfare dropped out of college. Moreover, due to past defaults on student loans or grants in the past, some welfare recipients may not be eligible for some federally funded financial aid programs.

Colleges might consider designating a staff person to help students on welfare navigate the financial aid system or develop written financial aid materials expressly for welfare recipients. In addition to basic information on scholarships and loans, welfare recipients need to know what the welfare office will provide and how to obtain welfare office assistance. For approved education and employment activities, welfare agencies typically provide financial help with child care expenses, transportation, books, and uniforms. Some agencies also cover registration or course fees. Unless welfare recipients are aware of these options, however, they may not think to ask.

Access to Program Information. Finally, simply not knowing about programs or their benefits can be a barrier to participation. Programs need to build strong relationships with their local welfare agency in order to ensure that welfare recipients are informed of community college options by their caseworkers. Colleges will likely also want to build strong referral relationships with workforce development and other public agencies, as well as local community-based organizations that are likely to serve the target population. Colleges might create marketing materials for their programs, such as posters, brochures, or videos that can be distributed at welfare offices and in the community. Partner agencies may include these materials in their planned mailings to clients, as welfare agencies in Maine and Kentucky have done.

Another way to strengthen existing referral relationships is for colleges to conduct training sessions for welfare or other agency staff about their welfare-to-work programs, so that caseworkers, receptionists, and others have more information to share with potential participants. College programs might even consider placing staff on-site at welfare agencies to conduct orientations and answer potential participants' questions about available programs and services. Colleges can work with welfare agencies to hold some activities at the college, such as job search, job club, or special events like job fairs, in order to familiarize welfare staff and recipients with the college campus and its resources.

Because not all welfare recipients are in frequent contact with their caseworkers, colleges will likely want to conduct outreach and marketing to potential participants in the community at large. Ideally, such outreach efforts will involve the college's central admissions office, as well as specialized welfare-to-work program offices. Colleges can also use current program participants as recruiters, even offering work-study slots as Riverside Community College's New Visions program has done (Fein, Beecroft, Long, and Catalfamo, 2000).

Seeking Out New Funding Opportunities. Some states, such as Washington, are applying TANF dollars to support program or curriculum development to create shorter-term programs that take time limits into account or to tailor programs to job opportunities in high-growth industries. Others, such as California and Kentucky, are using state TANF funds to create college-based case manager positions to assist welfare recipients with college-specific and personal support needs. TANF funds can also be used to support additional benefits and services, including tuition assistance, child care, transportation assistance, and state-level work-study programs.

Rather than rely on TANF funds alone, college welfare-to-work programs are in a unique position to merge these sources with additional federal, state, and local funding streams, leveraging additional resources. The U.S. Department of Labor Welfare-to-Work Grants program is not likely to be reauthorized, but there are a number of other federal funding sources for college-based welfare-to-work programs. College-based welfare-to-work programs may be able to tap into workforce development funding under the Workforce Investment Act. Specifically, college welfare-to-work programs might become partners in the one-stop centers that are being organized by many state and local workforce development agencies. The goal of these centers is to bring together a variety of federally funded employment and training services under one roof to improve coordination and facilitate access to services.

Some programs with an occupational training focus may be able to draw down funding from the Perkins Vocational and Technical Education Program. Colleges that provide vocational education are often eligible to receive Perkins grants through their state boards of vocational education and can use the funding to cover a variety of expenses, including equipment costs, curriculum design, career counseling, integrating academic and vocational education, staff, special services, and even remediation.

One new source of federal funding is the H1-B Technical Skills Training Grant awarded by the Department of Labor to local Workforce Investment Boards (WIBs) to support development of local training programs in high-skill technology areas that are facing labor shortages. Colleges can apply through their local WIBs for support; grants of up to $2.5 million have been awarded.

There are also private resources available to support welfare-to-work program efforts. Private foundations or other philanthropies may be willing to support program development or operations costs. Colleges can also work with the employers of working students to secure tuition reimbursement. For participants who are unemployed or seeking career advancement opportunities, colleges can partner with local employers to hire program graduates, fund and collaborate on program design and operations, donate equipment, and lend staff to serve as instructors or mentors.

Community Colleges and Welfare Recipients: A Good Fit

Colleges designing welfare-to-work programs face two seemingly conflicting goals: helping welfare recipients move into employment quickly and helping welfare recipients find and retain good jobs that have the potential for stability and living wages. As the Portland NEWWS site demonstrated, these goals are not necessarily incompatible; they can be achieved by developing individualized programs that combine job search with education and training and maintain a clear focus on employment. And there are many other ways community colleges can make their programs more flexible and attempt to build long-term relationships with clients so that they continue to work toward postsecondary educational goals after leaving welfare.

Compared to other institutions, community colleges offer several advantages as operators of welfare-to-work programs. They are accustomed to serving a wide range of students, from traditional college-aged students to older working students, and from various socioeconomic, racial, ethnic, and cultural backgrounds. They typically offer a wide menu of credit and noncredit academic, remedial, vocational, and continuing-education courses, as well as some campus-based support services. They can help participants acquire marketable credentials, including vocational certificates and associate degrees, and make the transition to four-year colleges and universities. Finally, they frequently have relationships with local employers, which they can use to provide job placement opportunities for welfare-to-work participants. Given these features, community colleges have the potential to set TANF recipients on a path toward reduced welfare dependence, increased employment opportunity, and economic gains.

Notes

1. Unless otherwise noted, the information in this section is adapted from Hamilton and others, 2001. NEWWS reports can be downloaded from either of the following Web sites: www.mdrc.org/WelfareReform/NEWWS.htm or aspe.hhs.gov/hsp/NEWWS/index.htm.
2. Unless otherwise noted, much of this section draws on information presented in Golonka and Matus-Grossman (2001).

References

Bos, J. M., Scrivener, S., Snipes, J., and Hamilton, G. *Improving Basic Skills: The Effects of Adult Education in Welfare-to-Work Programs.* Washington, D.C.: U.S. Department of Education, Office of the Under Secretary and Office of Vocational and Adult Education, and U.S. Department of Health and Human Services, Administration for Children and Families and Office of the Assistant Secretary for Planning and Evaluation, 2001.

Carnevale, A., and Desrochers, D. *Getting Down to Business: Matching Welfare Recipients' Skills to Jobs That Train.* Princeton, N.J.: Educational Testing Service, 1999.

Fein, D., Beecroft, E., Long, D. A., and Catalfamo, A. R. *The New Visions Evaluation: College as a Job Advancement Strategy: An Early Report on the New Visions Self-Sufficiency and Lifelong Learning Project.* Cambridge, Mass.: Abt Associates, 2000.

Freedman, S., and others. *Evaluating Alternative Welfare-to-Work Approaches: Two-Year Impacts for Eleven Programs.* Washington, D.C.: U.S. Department of Health and Human Services, Administration for Children and Families and Office of the Assistant Secretary for Planning and Evaluation, and U.S. Department of Education, Office of the Under Secretary and Office of Vocational and Adult Education, 2000.

Friedlander, D., and Burtless, G. *Five Years After: The Long Term Effects of Welfare-to-Work Programs.* New York: Russell Sage Foundation, 1995.

Golonka, S., and Matus-Grossman, L. *Opening Doors: Expanding Educational Opportunities for Low-Income Workers.* New York: Manpower Demonstration Research Corporation and National Governors Association Center for Best Practices, 2001.

Greenberg, M., Strawn, J., and Plimpton, L. *State Opportunities to Provide Access to Postsecondary Education Under TANF.* Washington, D.C.: Center for Law and Social Policy, 2000.

Grubb, W. N., Badway, N., Bell, D., and Castellano, M. "Community Colleges and Welfare Reform: Emerging Practices, Enduring Problems." Unpublished manuscript, School of Education, University of California, Berkeley, 1999.

Gueron, J. M., and Pauly, E. *From Welfare to Work.* New York: Russell Sage Foundation, 1991.

Hamilton, G., and Brock, T. *The JOBS Evaluation: Early Lessons from Seven Sites.* Washington, D.C.: U.S. Department of Health and Human Services, Administration for Children and Families and Office of the Assistant Secretary for Planning and Evaluation, and U.S. Department of Education, Office of the Under Secretary and Office of Vocational and Adult Education, 1994.

Hamilton, G., and others. *How Effective Are Different Welfare-to-Work Approaches? Five-Year Adult and Child Impacts for Eleven Programs.* Washington, D.C.: U.S. Department of Health and Human Services, Administration for Children and Families and Office of the Assistant Secretary for Planning and Evaluation, and U.S. Department of Education, Office of the Under Secretary and Office of Vocational and Adult Education, 2001.

Quint, J. C., Musick, J. S., and Ladner, J. A. *Lives of Promise, Lives of Pain: Young Mothers After New Chance.* New York: Manpower Demonstration Research Corporation, 1994.

U.S. General Accounting Office. *Work and Welfare: Current AFDC Work Programs and Implications for Federal Policy.* Washington, D.C.: General Accounting Office, 1987.

U.S. House of Representatives. Committee on Ways and Means. *Overview of Entitlement Programs: 1993 Green Book: Background Material and Data on Programs Within the Jurisdiction of the Committee on Ways and Means.* Washington, D.C.: U.S. Government Printing Office, 1993.

THOMAS BROCK *is senior research associate at the Manpower Demonstration Research Corporation, New York.*

LISA MATUS-GROSSMAN *is development analyst at the Manpower Demonstration Research Corporation, New York.*

GAYLE HAMILTON *is senior research associate at the Manpower Demonstration Research Corporation, New York.*

2

*In order for community colleges to fulfill their role in
welfare reform, careful attention must be paid to internal
and external constituencies. This chapter describes how
Modesto Junior College built partnerships based on trust
and mutual respect that led to success for welfare recipients.*

The Local Politics and Partnerships of Successful Welfare Reform at Modesto Junior College

Pamila J. Fisher

A community college's participation in welfare-to-work reform requires an institution to consider and conclude that such involvement is consistent with its mission. This discussion is the first step in the process of addressing internal politics and gaining the necessary support to develop and implement appropriate programs and services. Generally, leadership from the chancellor or president, as well as concurrence from the board of trustees, is essential to facilitating debate by the college's academic senate and other decision-making bodies.

Once the value of the community college's role in welfare reform has been accepted and integrated into the college mission, a consensus can be built with external partners. These partners include county offices of welfare or social services, employment and training departments, and other workforce development agencies. Similarly, close collaboration with state agencies in education, social services, and labor also is essential. Although federal welfare reform legislation has been in place for five years, community colleges also must maintain contact with their state and national associations and elected officials to pursue modifications to the law in order to serve constituents well.

Modesto Junior College (MJC) in California has followed these principles in building successful community college welfare-to-work programs. The college is an eighty-year-old comprehensive community college that

Major contributors to the content and programs described in this chapter include George Boodrookas, Jeff Jue, and Gerry Caviness.

serves approximately sixteen thousand students annually. It is located in Stanislaus County, a region with an economy largely based on agriculture. The region's population is highly diverse and home to a large number of immigrants. Stanislaus County historically has experienced double-digit unemployment that can reach 16 percent to 18 percent in the winter months. Not surprisingly, the number of persons on public assistance is very high, and the college has been a major provider of vocational programs, English as a Second Language, basic skills, and high school equivalency courses for the past twenty years. This chapter describes the planning and implementation of welfare-to-work programs at MJC under the requirements of Temporary Assistance to Needy Families (TANF), with a focus on the development of partnerships and collaborations.

Welfare to Work at MJC Prior to TANF

In 1986, the California legislature passed a welfare reform bill that created a new program, Greater Avenues for Independence (GAIN), designed to move people off public assistance and into gainful employment. This program proved to be a precursor, and to some extent a model, for the Personal Responsibility and Work Opportunity Reconciliation Act (PRWORA) welfare reform legislation passed by Congress in 1996 that established TANF.

Under GAIN, MJC had the largest community college welfare reform program in California for several years until the counties of Los Angeles and San Diego established their own programs. Even then, MJC remained the third largest in the state until the funding for GAIN ended in 1997. During this period, many community colleges chose not to get involved in the GAIN program. MJC did because it believed such involvement was consistent with its mission of serving all adults who could benefit from its programs. It served at least fifteen hundred students a year from 1988 through 1997, with a high of twenty-seven hundred in the final year of the program. By jointly offering programs with the county department of social services, the college was able to help the department meet matching fund requirements and gain greater access to funds.

The impact on the community was profound. The Stanislaus County Department of Social Services was recognized statewide for its outstanding success at reducing its welfare rolls. In spring 1997, the director of social services reported that welfare expenditures had been reduced by $11 million in 1995–1996 due to grant terminations or reductions as a result of employment and credited partnerships between MJC and the county with the success.

The collaboration that occurred in Stanislaus County for more than a decade required all parties involved to understand complex fiscal and programmatic regulations. It also required great trust and even more patience. I am convinced that GAIN programs worked well because all the players were strongly committed to their success. As Congress debated welfare reform in the mid-1990s, it was apparent that once again community leaders would need to work together to address the even larger challenge posed by the new programs.

Planning for TANF

In August 1996, Congress passed PRWORA, known informally as welfare reform. TANF is its major program that became effective in July 1997; the intervening year was one of much planning in communities across the country.

The State Level. Although California had a decade of experience with GAIN, it was not timely in its completion of a new state plan to meet the requirements of TANF. The state legislature had difficulty agreeing on regulations in areas where they had some discretion. Most of this disagreement centered on changes to the GAIN program that were fairly dramatic, such as time limits, opportunities for training, and the provision of support services.

The differences in opinion were apparent at a public summit hosted by the legislature in December 1996. Although there was agreement that California's economy needed a boost of skilled workers, there was little agreement on whether current welfare recipients could become those workers and even less on what it would take to make them acceptable to business and industry. As a participant in that summit, I returned to my community convinced that we needed to continue with our own preparations despite the ambiguity at the state level.

Several presidents and chancellors within the community college system shared these concerns and were involved in attempting to influence the structure of the California plan. As members of the Joint Commission on Federal Relations, we had worked to influence the federal legislation. Although we had not been entirely successful, we knew the legislation and understood that our next opportunity to affect the eventual outcome would be to influence the content of the state plan. In September 1996, I addressed the association of state community college chief executive officers with a set of recommendations urging colleagues to continue to educate their state legislators while also working closely with county officials.

The County Level. In Stanislaus County, numerous leaders were eager to improve the area's economy, increase the number of skilled workers, and decrease the welfare rolls to a greater extent than under the GAIN program. With the new federal regulations looming and the state regulations still being debated, county officials took the lead and formally began the local planning process. The county board of supervisors hosted a community summit on welfare reform in December 1996 with a cross section of several hundred community leaders. The purpose of the summit was to understand better the new welfare reform act, establish working relationships among community leaders and providers who serve families, and set in motion partnerships that would result in increased employment and solutions to meeting families' basic needs. The format included extensive discussion on the issues of jobs, training, child care, housing, medical care, and transportation. In the concluding session, it was stressed that California would need to invest heavily in welfare reform to prevent a major economic and social disaster.

Educators from the K–12 districts and the community college were key players in this summit and in the activities that followed. One of the most visible of these was the formation of a welfare reform steering committee, comprising representatives from welfare, medical services, mental health, housing, law enforcement, transportation, child care, community nonprofit organizations, economic development, and education. As a member of this committee, I was able to stay well connected with the leadership, and we shared information, ideas, and resources. In addition, our respective staffs in each area worked even more closely as they designed solutions to the problems our mutual clients faced. We were particularly effective in acquiring grants that enabled us to expand our programs.

For four years, the steering committee met monthly. We still meet for the same purposes, although it is no longer necessary to meet as frequently. Nevertheless, the communication bridges are so strong that it is easy to reach one another and solve problems as they arise, often within hours or days. The theme of building relationships and maintaining collaboration toward a common cause has become a value and has been institutionalized.

The College Level. Even as this activity was occurring at the county and state levels, more was happening on campus. We were preparing for what would become an even larger set of programs and services specifically designed for college students who were TANF recipients. The staff was committed to helping the people affected by these changes and made great efforts to ensure student survival and success.

An early step was keeping the staff leadership well informed so that the new legislation did not surprise our institution. Our next step was to inform all staff of the implications for our college. I explained components of the new law and shared statistics about our students and the local population to our college community. I highlighted the many challenges these people would face and identified those with which we could assist. And I emphasized why it was our ethical obligation to help these community members be successful, even if we had to change the way we operated.

For example, we would need to expand our ESL, basic education, and specific vocational training programs. We would need to offer these programs in shorter time frames and in a wider variety of nontraditional formats. Because the TANF students would be required to meet a work obligation in addition to their studies, we would need to increase campus opportunities in work-study, cooperative work experience, internships, and other work-related activities. I also predicted that the demand for campus child care, as well as trained child care providers throughout the community, would grow dramatically. All these ideas, and many more, were embraced, expanded, and implemented.

The following month, I called on the presidents of each college in our district to form a college welfare reform task force. Their charge was to become familiar with the law, the statistics, and the issues and identify how the college could respond. Because of the ambiguity that still existed, I prepared a list of planning assumptions that guided their work. The most important of these was that we would do whatever was necessary to retain the more than twenty-five hundred GAIN (and soon to be TANF) students who were enrolled. I asked them to do that based on their existing budgets and to identify how they would spend additional funding should the state make that available. Each task force was asked to make monthly reports during the spring of 1997 and be prepared to implement at least part of their plan by the fall.

An early activity of the MJC task force was working with the academic senate and the curriculum committee to adopt a request for proposal process. They solicited ideas for new short-term offerings in the areas of basic skills, soft job skills (interpersonal skills, behaviors, attitudes, and communication styles), and modifications to existing vocational certificate programs. Criteria, examples, and information sessions were provided, and collaboration between and among vocational and liberal arts faculty was strongly encouraged. Perhaps most important, a $2,500 grant for each accepted proposal was offered.

By the fall of 1997, we knew that in addition to any services that the college might provide on a contract basis with the Department of Social Services, funding for serving TANF students would be available through the California Community Colleges Chancellor's Office based on new state legislation. This funding was not universally celebrated throughout the community college system because it came from a source that otherwise would have gone to the community colleges as discretionary funds. However, once the legislature had made that decision, colleges that had been serving GAIN students were prepared to serve TANF students. The formula for the funding allocation initially was based on the number of welfare recipient students who had been enrolled in 1996. Thus, MJC was well positioned to embark on an expanded program as long as we could deliver it within a few months.

Welfare Reform Implementation at MJC

When California finally passed legislation to implement the federal welfare reform package, it was known as CalWORKs (California Work Opportunity and Responsibility to Kids). When Stanislaus County developed its local plan for welfare reform implementation, it adopted the name StanWORKs. The StanWORKs plan reflects the collaboration and cooperation between the Department of Social Services and MJC that had existed for the prior ten

years. Throughout the StanWORKs document are references to the antici-
pated contributions from and partnerships with the college. The plan makes
it clear that in order to provide needed services and reduce the number of
persons receiving public assistance, the department will rely on collaborative efforts and eliminate duplication of services.

It is noteworthy that in the first program objective listed in the plan,
there is reference to creating partnerships with several other entities, including educational institutions and training providers. Existing providers of
services in basic literacy, vocational training, and postsecondary education
are listed, and MJC is mentioned in each category. The plan also outlines
existing and prospective partnerships with local business and industry. Since
the plan was adopted, partnerships with other institutes and academies have
been developed in response to specific employment opportunities.

The college serves TANF students in many programs throughout the
entire college. Some are enrolled in traditional programs supplemented with
work experience and work-study opportunities. Some are enrolled in intensive shorter-length vocational programs. Many are enrolled in basic skills,
high school equivalency courses, and adult basic education. Hundreds more
are benefiting from the Job Club (which helps candidates identify, apply, and
interview for jobs) and other assistance programs that the college offers off
campus. On campus, student services staff provide counseling, tutoring, dis-
ability services, and other programs designed to help students achieve success. Campus child care facilities and programs have quadrupled in the past
three years. These varied services are being provided on the college campus,
in sites around the county, and in several locations called one-stop centers.
Currently, the number of TANF participants at MJC is approaching three
thousand.

Examples of specialized programs and services being offered include
the following. Open entry–open exit courses are offered in ESL, general educational development, and other basic skills areas in compute-assisted labs
that contain ninety individual stations, each with numerous software pack-
ages. A separate office administration laboratory provides a variety of office
administration curricula in an open entry format. Specialized programs
include a culinary arts academy, landscape and nursery aide training for
minimum security prisoners, a bilingual industrial technology program, and
a preconstruction skill training program that is a joint effort with minority
community-based organizations and the local building industry association.

A number of MJC offerings assist students with their job performance.
Job Track promotes job retention after employment begins. The New
Employee Mentoring Program pairs new employees with a mentor at their
place of employment. Extensive work-study is offered both on and off campus, primarily for students with limited English and limited work experience. The college also received an AmeriCorps National Service Program
grant. Up to fifty AmeriCorps members, who are college child development
majors and TANF recipients, serve as tutors for preschool age children.

Another thirty AmeriCorps students mentor local youth through the college's human services program.

The Workforce Training Center's role has expanded outside the college. It was asked to provide training to other providers involved in welfare reform programs. For example, there are approximately a dozen agencies represented at the one-stop centers. MJC was asked to provide training to all the agency staff so that they would be effective members of the one-stop team. MJC staff also worked with Department of Social Services staff to produce materials used to respond to the needs of students coping with domestic violence. In demonstration of the trust and respect between the two entities, MJC now offers an evening college program at the Department of Social Services, which awards a certificate or associate degree program on site to the department's staff.

Early results of Stanislaus County's StanWORKs program are encouraging. Although the caseload had been reduced significantly in the last years of GAIN, another drop occurred in the first three and a half years of StanWORKs. Specifically, the caseload was reduced by another 32 percent, and by the year 2000 the caseload had been reduced by more than 45 percent. Program expenditures were reduced by 50 percent, saving almost $50 million a year. In the first three years of the program, an average of forty-one hundred former welfare recipients gained employment each year. Recently, the placement rate has declined to about three thousand per year as the program serves more clients with multiple barriers to success. Comments from graduates consistently reflect a new sense of self-esteem, commitment to their children's education, and optimism about the future. These successes are attributed to a focus on work and lifelong learning, an emphasis on the theme of personal responsibility, and the many collaborative partnerships.

Partnerships and Collaboration

I recently asked several of the key players from MJC and the county Community Services Agency to comment on the partnerships that have evolved between the two agencies. All agreed that the excellent working relationships are the outcome of years of experience in addressing and resolving challenges. The leadership and staff in both agencies remain committed to the goals of the welfare-to-work program.

The director of the Workforce Training Center commented that "both agencies have been open, candid and forthcoming about concerns and constraints." He went on to say that the high trust level from the respective agency leadership allowed staff to develop relationships where they could develop successful programs "despite regulations, time limits, restrictions and client barriers to success." The director of the Community Services Agency pointed out that this model for interagency partnership is exemplified in the trust that made possible the combining of fiscal resources. He said that the "leveraging and braiding of funds enhanced service capacity and allowed creative programs to emerge." He was especially impressed that the synergy of this partnership "facilitated an accelerated progress of moving from concept to implementation in some instances in only a matter of weeks or months."

The value of the partnerships that resulted from this relationship is summarized in a comment from the assistant director of the Community Services Agency. She stated that the outstanding working relationship with MJC over the past ten years can be "attributed in large part to the integrity, professionalism and collaborative spirit of staff from both agencies. Each has shown a willingness to tackle difficult issues honestly and openly with the mutual goal of meeting the needs of our customers and community."

As is true for counties and community colleges across the country, serious barriers remain as TANF recipients attempt to gain the skills necessary to obtain gainful employment. Regulations on time limits and access to education and training, and emphasizing work first, even when the salary is barely above or even below the poverty level, all work to the disadvantage of some students. It will be necessary for all concerned parties to press elected officials to modify existing regulations if welfare reform is to continue to be successful. This is especially true as the clients who remain on the welfare rolls today are likely to need more attention and be less ready for employment.

Fortunately, where strong partnerships and successful track records exist, the advocates for change will be more likely to wield influence on state and national policymakers. The local politics of welfare reform are indeed a function of relationships. Where positive and productive relationships exist, the political field can be navigated and good policy adopted and implemented. In Stanislaus County, we have a fifteen-year track record of collaboration, partnerships, and success. We are confident that by working together, we will meet and then exceed any new challenge just as we have met them in the past.

PAMILA J. FISHER *is chancellor of the Yosemite Community College District and chair of the board of directors of the American Association of Community Colleges.*

3

This chapter discusses community colleges and welfare to work from a rural perspective, specifically in Illinois. It examines the barriers to rural welfare recipients in terms of job placement, the benefits of collaborative efforts and partnerships, and the importance of education and training.

The State of Welfare Reform in the Rural Communities of Illinois

Kathleen Vespa Pampe

Illinois began implementation of Temporary Aid for Needy Families (TANF) on July 1, 1997, replacing Aid to Families with Dependent Children. The Illinois program includes work requirements, time-limited assistance, family stability through improved child support enforcement, personal and parental responsibility, and improved data reporting. Specific TANF initiatives include the Targeted Work Initiative (TWI), which is for families with no children under the age of thirteen, and the Work Pays program, which provides financial incentives for clients who find jobs. Both programs continue supportive services after employment, depending on salary. Teenage parents who do not have a high school diploma or general educational development (GED) must earn the diploma or GED and must cooperate with the Teen Parent Services Program (Illinois Department of Human Services, 2000). Local personnel from the state Department of Human Services (DHS) work individually with clients to complete a responsibility and services plan that outlines specific education and employment goals, including barriers and supportive service requirements (Illinois Department of Human Services, 2000).

What has the new welfare system and the subsequent mandate for jobs meant to education and particularly to Illinois community colleges that work closely with welfare agencies in providing education and training? TANF has decreased the emphasis on education and training, therefore directly affecting colleges' enrollments, as well as programs and services targeted to welfare recipients. Community college educators have also been skeptical of a system that mandates work for individuals without providing them with the prerequisite skills through education and training. To Illinois

NEW DIRECTIONS FOR COMMUNITY COLLEGES, no. 116, Winter 2001 © John Wiley, & Sons, Inc.

educators, it seemed that the work-first plan ensured failure for welfare clients and promoted the deemphasis of workforce preparation and education. However, according to *Illinois Welfare News,* the "percentage of recipients 'in school' decreased from 11 to 9 percent" only (Bouman, 2001, p. 2).

Illinois Community Colleges and Welfare to Work

Illinois is a large and diverse state. Its 102 counties have varied demographic and economic profiles. Aside from Chicago, the largest urban area in Illinois with the largest number of welfare caseloads, Illinois is primarily rural, with midsize cities like Peoria, East St. Louis, Bloomington, Kankakee, Springfield, and Chicago suburbs in Cook and Dupage counties interspersed. Illinois has the third largest community college system in the country, with thirty-nine community college districts and forty-eight community colleges. These colleges serve 60 percent of all undergraduate students enrolled in public higher education in the state, including over 750,000 students in credit classes and approximately 250,000 students in noncredit classes (Illinois Community College System, 2001). Illinois community colleges have also been very instrumental in helping low-income people attain educational goals that subsequently lead to new or improved career plans and quality-of-life issues.

Illinois community colleges have a long and successful history of collaboration with the Illinois DHS in promoting education and special programs that help move people off welfare and into jobs that pay more than minimum wage. In fact, for almost ten years, thirty of the state's forty-eight community colleges within the Illinois system operated under a $4.1 million contract, with the DHS providing approximately thirty-two hundred students per year with education, training, and special services. But TANF and the work-first priority have forced Illinois, its counties, and its community colleges to plan and collaborate differently.

Soon after implementation, TANF showed early signs of success in reducing the numbers of welfare recipients. In 1994, the nation's welfare rolls were estimated at 14.3 million. By September 2000, the rolls had decreased by over 60 percent, with fewer than 5.8 million people listed as welfare recipients (U.S. Department of Health and Human Services, 1999). Illinois reported a similar strong decline, with a 79.8 percent reduction in welfare caseloads between September 1994 and March 2001 (Illinois Department of Human Services, 2001). However, it is important to note that during the first few years of TANF implementation, the economy was booming, with unemployment figures at an all-time low particularly for many Illinois counties with an average of 4 percent unemployment statewide (Illinois Department of Employment Security, 2001a). Also noteworthy is that although a large number of recipients left TANF, there was no evidence that they had gotten jobs (Bouman, 2001).

It became apparent during the first few years of implementation that there were several classifications or categories of welfare recipients. Individuals in the first category were very employable, may have already had a job or alternative income, or had an education ranging from a high school diploma to a college degree and did not want to contend with the stricter policies and procedures to retain the minimal cash assistance they received. The second category included individuals who possessed some job skills, had a high school–level education or diploma, and with assistance for child care and transportation could obtain jobs. The third category of individuals, many of whom remain on the rolls, lack education, specifically a GED or high school diploma, and lack basic life skills or work skills preparation. This group also has serious barriers to jobs and education, such as learning disabilities, substance abuse problems, and prison records, as well as the typical child care and transportation problems. It is this group about whom state officials are most concerned and that raises questions about whether those who could leave the rolls already have done so ("Welfare Caseloads Begin to Rise," 2001).

Illinois Eastern Community Colleges District

Illinois Eastern Community Colleges (IECC), in the most southeastern part of the state, is one of only two multicollege districts in Illinois; City Colleges of Chicago has seven colleges and Illinois Eastern has four (Frontier, Lincoln Trail, Olney Central, and Wabash Valley). IECC's district covers all or parts of thirteen counties, an area of approximately three thousand square miles, is very rural, and is economically depressed. When the state's unemployment figures were at 4 percent, several counties in the IECC District held double-digit unemployment figures (Illinois Department of Employment Security, 2001b). The largest city in the district has a population of about ninety-one hundred people, a large expanse of land with the population sparsely distributed. Most of the cities throughout southeastern Illinois are accessed by a two-lane highway system with access to an interstate highway over an hour away in any direction; the largest metropolitan cities are two to three hours away in travel time.

There are pockets of industry, meaning there are just a few towns throughout the district housing industry that support large employment. Nearly half of the district's population (47 percent) is designated as low-income families, with one of the larger counties, Richland County, listing over 19 percent of children falling below poverty levels (U.S. Census Bureau, 1999). Education rates for the counties and the district are equally low. For example, in Clay and Richland counties, 20 percent of the population aged twenty-five years and over have less than a ninth-grade education and 35 percent of the population do not have a high school diploma or GED (U.S. Census Bureau, 1999). Recently, one of the larger employers in the IECC district laid off over three-fourths of its workforce. Over half these workers tested below seventh-grade reading and math levels.

There is no mass transit and only limited special transportation. Most of the jobs that would be accessible to individuals with limited education, such as retail and fast food, are sparse, and due to a slowing economy throughout the district, industry jobs are at a minimum and generally require fairly high skill levels.

Collaboration and Coordination under TANF

For rural areas, TANF presents special challenges not only for welfare recipients but also for state and county officials who are trying to meet the plan and the plan's mandates. These challenges can be met only through strong collaboration and coordination of resources, and rural southern Illinois counties and community colleges provide effective examples of collaboration and coordination.

For southern Illinois, statistics show not only the rural nature and poverty of the area but also the additional barriers and challenges social service agencies and community colleges must face in order to work with residents and clients. DHS county offices and community colleges are also faced with the dilemma that those remaining on the rolls have severe educational and work barriers. Although IECC has not been involved with the DHS and the community college state contract program, it has been the recipient of a small grant program from the Illinois Community College Board. The grant program has provided funding for a position that serves as a liaison among the colleges, the local DHS county offices, and the other social service agencies. Prior to the grant program and the liaison, communication between the colleges and the local offices was not strong, and collaboration was almost nonexistent. With the efforts of the liaison visiting all the DHS local offices on a regular basis, resources have been expanded and better used for the benefit of clients most in need, and funding for all clients has been expanded through collaboration of funds.

Referrals to community college programs and services, primarily adult education programs, have greatly increased, as have referrals to classes on life and work skills. Better information about the programs and services offered by the IECC has promoted new programs and services, and information from the local DHS offices has helped the colleges identify needs such as more short-term certificates and better testing and assessment. The district has created several new certificate programs and is also going to pilot a program that will loan laptop computers to welfare recipients so they can access college-level classes on-line from home. If successful, the program will provide great educational opportunities and access to higher education throughout IECC's rural communities and is one educational solution relative to transportation and child care problems. The district also hired a state-certified assessment specialist who identifies learning problems and disabilities and provides methods, planning, programs, and devices for meeting the problems and disabilities. Often the learning problem is simply the need for eyeglasses, a hearing aid, or a special ruler that helps an individual read a printed page. The district, in collaboration with funding from local DHS offices, has used various grant programs to purchase these tools. Local DHS staff and other social service agency staff plan to use the specialized testing and assessment programs and the assessment specialist's expertise to better prepare clients for education and jobs.

The district and the local DHS offices are planning to collaborate on the use of the American College Testing (ACT) Work Keys Assessments for welfare clients, with IECC becoming a testing center that includes job profiling and job analysis. ACT Work Keys "is a national system for teaching and assessing workplace skills that connects knowing with doing and learning with earning" (American College Testing, 1994). These skill assessments represent basic workplace skills that have been identified by business and industry and education skills required for current and new entrants into the workplace. There are eight workplace assessments: applied mathematics, applied technology, listening, locating information, observation, reading for information, teamwork, and writing. Many of the district's industries, high schools, and IECC have been using the ACT Work Keys Assessments for the past couple of years. In fact, Illinois high schools implemented a new statewide test for high school students that includes two of the ACT Work Keys Assessments in reading and mathematics (Illinois State Board of Education, 2000).

Another program, Worldwide Interactive Network (WIN), serves as a remediation program. WIN is a series of thirty-six levels of competency-based instruction designed specifically for all eight ACT Work Keys Assessments. WIN meets the Secretary's Commission on Achieving Necessary Skills (SCANS) objectives and is designed to meet workforce literacy initiatives. For example, if a student is at a level two or three and a job profile requires a level five or six, this program will aid in raising assessment scores. WIN is both a CD-based and book form program. IECC's Adult Education Program plans to begin using WIN as a pretest for the development and remediation of workplace skills. Also, the welfare-to-work liaison will administer the WIN program to clients at the local DHS offices.

IECC also houses the Illinois Employment and Training Center (IETC), with on-site partnership and assistance from the Illinois Department of Employment Security, the welfare-to-work program, the local Workforce Investment Board staff, and rotating agency staff, including the Teen Parent Services Program and Office of Rehab Services. The IETC provides direct access to economic development agencies, businesses, and industries throughout the district, which leads to better identification of and access to jobs for welfare clients.

In discussions with local DHS personnel, area employers have been very receptive to hiring welfare recipients, and for the most part, many successes have been realized. However, work with employers and clients helped identify an additional need: job retention services, and particularly job coaches. IECC is examining the possibility of adding job coaching to its list of services, which would provide one-on-one on-site job mentoring for newly employed individuals. The IECC Adult Education Program has also developed an employability skills class that is being promoted to welfare recipients to help them retain jobs. The course covers topics such as resumè writing, computer job search, interviewing, career interest inventories, work ethic, teamwork, and customer service. Each student will complete the class with a personal portfolio that he or she can present to potential employers. In an effort to help welfare recipients to dress professionally, the IETC has opened the Career Clothing Closet, which provides men and women free clothing for job interviews and starting jobs. Donations have come from all over the IECC district.

Transportation continues to be a major problem in this rural area. Through various grant programs and again including collaboration of funds with local DHS offices, clients are provided gas and car repair vouchers and, in a few instances, funds to purchase a used vehicle, but so far, this has helped very few individuals compared to the large numbers needing transportation. The district and the social service agencies wrote a grant proposal that would provide funding to purchase vans and buses enabling the transport of greater numbers of people to and from work and education. Although that grant was not funded, agencies and colleges are still working together toward the development of a transportation plan and will work more closely with county officials, emphasizing the need for transportation throughout several southern Illinois counties.

TANF is up for federal reauthorization in 2002, and like any other reauthorization, there could be major changes to the program and funding. Several local DHS staff believe the changes will be centered on the five-year time limits. And this will come at a time when many individuals will be facing that time limit. Overall, according to local agency staff and community college staff, TANF seems to be effective in helping people move off the welfare rolls into jobs, appropriate educational programs, and specific services for those with severe needs.

Conclusion

In southeastern Illinois, individuals are being placed into jobs and are receiving education and training. In this rural region, collaboration and coordination of resources between social service agencies and the community colleges have been enhanced and expanded, and the welfare rolls in Illinois continue to decline ("Welfare Caseloads Begin to Rise," 2001).

Workforce preparation and training for all of IECC's residents will continue to be a major emphasis, particularly with the increasing challenge of decreasing economic growth and stability. IECC, in continued collaboration with numerous partners, will promote education in order to decrease poverty and the need for welfare.

References

American College Testing. *Work Keys.* Iowa City: American College Testing Publications, 1994.

Bouman, J. "TANF Turns 4—One More Year Until Time Limit Kicks In: Challenges for Next Phases of Welfare and Work Force Reform." *Illinois Welfare News,* 2001, *11,* 1–9.

Illinois Community College System. *Facts About Community Colleges.* Springfield: Illinois Community College System, 2001.

Illinois Department of Employment Security. *Illinois Labor Force Report.* Springfield: Illinois Department of Employment Security, 2001a.

Illinois Department of Employment Security. *Local Area Unemployment Statistics.* Springfield: Illinois Department of Employment Security, 2001b.

Illinois Department of Human Services. *Temporary Assistance for Needy Families.* Springfield: Illinois Department of Human Services Publications, 2001.

Illinois State Board of Education. *Prairie State Achievement Exam.* Springfield: Illinois State Board of Education, 2000.

U.S. Census Bureau. *USA Counties.* Washington, D.C.: U.S. Department of Commerce, 1999.

U.S. Department of Health and Human Services. *Temporary Assistance for Needy Families (TANF) Program: Second Annual Report to Congress.* Washington, D.C.: U.S. Department of Health and Human Services, 1999.

U.S. Department of Labor. *Learning a Living: A Blueprint for High Performance: A SCANS Report for America 2000, Part I.* Washington, D.C.: U.S. Government Printing Office, 1992.

"Welfare Caseloads Begin to Rise." *Olney* (Ill.) *Daily Mail,* Apr. 4, 2001, p. 1.

KATHLEEN VESPA PAMPE *is associate dean for career education and economic development, Illinois Eastern Community Colleges.*

4

This chapter focuses on the experiences and lessons learned from the effort by Wisconsin Moraine Park Technical College to develop a welfare-to-work program and emphasizes the importance of having a strong workforce-readiness component in the training program.

The Transition to Work First in a Wisconsin Technical College

Dennis H. Nitschke

Wisconsin has gained the reputation as one of the nation's leading states in implementing welfare reform. Among the major efforts legislated in the mid- to late 1990s were Work Not Welfare (WNW), Wisconsin Works (W-2), and Partnership for Full Employment. The technical colleges were concerned that most of this legislation, except WNW, reduced the role of the job training and retention training. Technical colleges had a two-year window of opportunity to pilot short-term training initiatives immediately before Wisconsin made its dramatic transition to W-2. This time period was from January 1995 to January 1997 and was driven by state legislation WNW.

Work Not Welfare in Wisconsin

Like other states, Wisconsin did not wait for federal legislation to mandate welfare reform. Wisconsin's welfare reform efforts with its WNW initiative made national news between January 1995 and January 1997. Many view this period as the transition between the period prior to 1995, when community colleges enjoyed funding for class-size projects and full-time student program enrollment under the Job Training Partnership Act (JTPA) and the train-then-work model, to the fully implemented W-2 welfare initiative and the work-first model in 1997.

The WNW initiative that began on January 1, 1995, was widely held to be the nation's first welfare reform initiative that required work in exchange for benefits. It limited recipients to a maximum of twenty-four months on the program to receive cash welfare benefits. As a comprehensive approach to welfare reform, WNW provided temporary cash assistance, job training and job placement, child care, health care, and transportation support to encourage and enable welfare recipients to make the transition to work and self-sufficiency.

The two counties in Wisconsin selected to pilot the WNW initiative were given additional funding and were empowered to be creative in addressing the challenges. It was understood that the state would learn from these pilot counties and incorporate key concepts into future W-2 legislation. Governor Tommy Thompson selected Pierce County (in northwest Wisconsin) and Fond du Lac County (one of ten counties within the Moraine Park Technical College District located in east-central Wisconsin) to pilot this initiative. Each county was required to form a community steering committee to coordinate the public-private partnership necessary to match individuals with local employment opportunities.

The technical colleges serving these two counties were invited to be a major community partner in this transition process. Although the colleges welcomed this opportunity, it also presented difficulties; there was a significant negative association with the dramatic reductions in the traditionally strong JTPA-funded enrollments, and the colleges were being asked to customize and modularize short-term training for WNW participants.

Outcomes for Moraine Park Technical College

Two of Yogi Berra's famous quotes come to mind: "the future, it ain't what it used to be" and "nothing changes if nothing changes." The staff at Moraine Park Technical College (MPTC) in Fond du Lac County realized that the future role it must play in publicly funded workforce training would be different than it had been in the past. The question was what impact MPTC could have during this piloted WNW program. How could the college influence policymakers to embrace training as a vital part of this reform and recognize how creative and responsive two-year colleges can be in meeting this challenge? At the end of the pilot, the result was not positive: there was very little impact on the final W-2 legislation regarding the role of short-term training. The WNW legislation, however, did present MPTC with a unique opportunity to pilot new and creative short-term training initiatives and to take risks and feel empowered.

Employer-Driven Needs. The local chamber of commerce conducted a survey of employers to determine the most critical community employment needs. This information played a major role in designing approaches to interviewing, assessing, and employability planning and designing the nature and length of training required. The survey results also indicated the need for greater employer focus on training and coaching activities. The college heard employers clearly state that the most critical skill that new employees needed was to be generally prepared for the workplace environment.

Related Certificates. MPTC customized a series of one- to twelve-week training programs and awarded certificates for those who completed them. Not only was this meaningful to the individual participants, but the training was deemed valuable to employers, and there were applications of this training in the private lives of the participants as well.

Career Ladder and Transcripted Credits. A barrier for some community colleges is the ability to deliver partial credits at the associate degree level and to have these cumulative credits apply toward other college certificates or programs. In Wisconsin, the technical colleges are permitted to do just that. The receipt of a transcript, even for seven and a half credits in a short-term training program, added significant value and validity to the training for both the participant and the employer.

Through this experience, MPTC staff learned a series of new paradigms that have application in other training, partnering, and community change initiatives:

• *Change through welfare reform must follow more of an agricultural change model than a mechanical change model.* In a mechanical change model, efforts focus on such factors as trying to fix the people because there is something wrong; telling the participants they must try harder but without making significant changes in the support systems; establishing only short-term traditional measures of success; maintaining a management philosophy of control, in which the county Department of Social Services has all of the authority; and spreading blame to others (individuals, agencies, and the state).

In the preferred agricultural change model, efforts focus on recognizing that behaviors, attitudes, and paradigms must be changed; understanding that welfare reform is a community problem requiring broad systemic change; identifying long- and short-term measures of success; placing authority with the community steering committee to influence the change process along with social services; structuring activities toward accountability as opposed to tightening the control mechanisms; and focusing on solutions rather than blame.

• *Involvement in welfare reform must be viewed as an economic development initiative rather than a social reengineering initiative.* Having the proper long-term vision and mission for those involved in the change (welfare recipients as well as community partners) was essential for the necessary decision-making processes, development of measures of success, and sustainability of critical community partner involvement—businesses in particular. Employers would not remain committed unless there was some return to what was deemed important to their livelihood, and that was to build and maintain a prepared workforce for the community. The challenge was not simply to move people from not working to the world of work. It was moving them in a meaningful way to self-sufficiency as well as meeting the workforce needs to move the community forward. This success was to be measured in new ways, such as how success is defined by the participants and their new employer rather than simply the percentage drop in welfare roles.

The college must identify the key customers in this welfare reform initiative and seek to serve these customers in new and responsive ways. MPTC identified three key customers: the country Department of Social Services, the WNW clients, and the employers.

The county Department of Social Services, which understood the welfare laws—previous Aid to Families with Dependent Children (AFDC) laws as well as the new WNW legislation—was designated to lead the reform. It was the agency through which related funding moved, and it coordinated all contacts with participants moving off AFDC who would benefit from participation in the college's customized WNW training activities.

The WNW clients were considered at risk and in need of the college's best training resources. One of MPTC's trainers put it best when she said her first and probably most important roles were to be a caring and connecting mentor. It was essential that the college did everything in its power to make certain WNW clients were not being blamed for the situations resulting in their attending the training; make certain WNW clients were not feeling like victims with the sense that all choice and self-esteem were taken from them; and make certain that all resources of the community (supportive services, staff, and fiscal) were properly aligned to support the individual client needs during this period of transition and change.

Finally, if welfare reform was viewed by the community as directly linked to economic development and the workforce, then employers' involvement and their customized training needs to meet their workforce requirements had to be a priority. It was the employer community that began to change their approach to hiring new workers. Rather than telling MPTC to push participants through short-term training, employers became personally involved in screening, training, coaching, and supporting participants.

The Nature of Short-Term Training

The three college-identified customers—the Department of Social Services, WNW clients, and area employers—caused the college to redefine its instructional roles and its measures of success, base of power, and depth and breadth of relationships. MPTC serves over twenty-four thousand headcount students annually, is accredited by the North Central Accrediting Association, delivers programs approved by the Wisconsin Technical College System Board, employs faculty who meet carefully prescribed state certification standards, and is recognized by area businesses for its strong customized training capacity. The college thought it had the complete answer to WNW short-term training issues.

MPTC had a food service and a culinary arts program with an active program advisory committee and felt confident that its staff understood what competencies the new ten-week training should address. A short-term training group was created consisting of employers, social services staff, other training organizations, and outside advisers. The college presented what it thought would be the appropriate competencies and curriculum but found that it would have significantly missed the mark. The overwhelming need was for soft skills (communications, interpersonal behaviors, teamwork, and problem solving). The short-term training group wanted at least 60 percent of the training to focus on development of soft skills. Employers said they would commit to training the occupational competencies and sending employed workers back to MPTC if new workers showed up for work three days in a row, were productive when they arrived at work, and could get along with coworkers and their supervisor.

This employer response was a result of the high staff turnover rates and cost of poor performance of some of their current workforce, not a direct reflection on the WNW training participants. They expressed their need, and clearly. The college took time to listen carefully to an expanded source of stakeholders and then acted, in cooperation with social services and employers, to modify the curriculum, support system, and accountability measures for these short-term training programs.

Part of the college's overall response was to clarify several key definitions. There was an obvious difference between the terms *job readiness* and *work readiness* that needed to be addressed. *Job readiness* indicates preparation of an individual for a particular job. The need for job readiness occurs several times in an individual's career and can result from technology changes, promotion, career change, and other factors. *Work readiness* indicates preparation of an individual for the general working world—in other words, having the required soft skills. Employers and others were telling the college that job readiness without work readiness was a sure guarantee for failure for both the employee and employer. Once work ready, employees could learn on the job and learn job-ready skills in a variety of ways.

Two additional definitions were developed and used during this WNW period. The terms *education* and *training* were often used interchangeably, so the following definitions were developed: *education* is just-in-case knowledge and is similar to a suitcase on a long trip (you should have enough clothes to last you for a while); *training* is just-in-time or just enough knowledge and is similar to a carry-on bag on a trip (you must pick up more clothing when you arrive).

The traditional college model was to package employer and participant needs into sixteen-week semesters, one- to three-hour class periods, three credit modules, and on-campus instruction with full-time faculty, focusing primarily on the occupational competencies. Now the college was being directed to deliver behavior-changing training, in time blocks of six hours per day over a ten-week period, using a combination of part-time and business trainers, involving extensive field trips and employment-related experiences. In addition, Department of Social Services staff would be active and visible in supporting related participant needs, such as transportation, child care, and health needs. To some degree, MPTC was experiencing firsthand that it was not just the welfare recipient who was being asked to change; the college's instructional paradigm was being challenged. Being outside the comfort zone affected the college in many ways.

The new requirement was for some college policies and procedures to be flexible rather than judging effectiveness on traditional adherence to existing policies and procedures. Because new curriculum and delivery methods had to be created for this initiative, the traditional instructional turf of departments and faculty had to be amended. The blending of sources to fund these new training initiatives required the college to become more flexible and creative in how it developed and managed budgets. Finally, the fear of change had to be recognized as a barrier to this initiative, driven partially by the loss of the JTPA funding and the loss of enrollment due to WNW.

Between 1995 and 1997, the college piloted and modified a number of different training efforts. During the first year, MPTC attempted to customize its offerings to serve WNW participants but had not yet effectively listened to the participants and employers. It attempted to make minor modifications to existing curriculum and courses and did not in fact customize the short-term training to meet the specific needs of participants and employers. The result was moderate success, with half of the participants completing the training. In the second year, there were significant changes in the content and delivery methodology as reflected in the earlier explanation of changes made to the hospitality and housekeeping training. The results in the second year showed considerable improvement, with an 80 percent completion rate, which represented a 30 percent increase over the first year.

Key Improvements in Training in Year 2

The improved participant completion rates in year 2 stemmed from a wide variety of improvements over year 1:

• The focus of training changed to soft skills and job retention skills, not job training. It was not so much an intellectual exercise as it was one of the trainer's caring, connecting, and mentoring participants.

• The college incorporated the workplace skills assessment (pre- and posttraining) to document changes and levels of ability in these work-keeping skill competencies. The results were used to modify curriculum, establish a benchmark to measure student progress, and create a hidden transcript that participants could use with prospective employers.

• Businesses took on an expanded, visible role to pull the participants toward employment. This was a new role for most employers, who were used to "catching" students off the education and training line (a shift from supply-side hiring to demand-side hiring).

• A one-week workshop on self-esteem building was piloted prior to the formal training program, with positive results. This workshop helped participants understand the requirements and changes associated with WNW and established a connection with other participants and with the college. This workshop served to welcome the participants as MPTC students and introduced them to the requirements of WNW, the resources that the college offered, and other participants. In essence, WNW was not something being done to them; it was being done with them and through them.

• The aspect of promoting cross-training and skill building in multiple areas within a given occupational area was part of all training. This activity focused more on developing the concept of skill security, not solely job security, and gave participants greater opportunities for employment in the future.

• A series of work-related certificates were built into the training programs, such as cardiopulmonary resuscitation and first aid, the national sanitation and safety certificate, customer service, and fire extinguisher training. This training (for example, emergency first aid, how to put out smaller fires, and general sanitation knowledge) had application at home as well as at the workplace. It also provided additional credentials for the interview with prospective employers.

• At least five days of workplace tours were led by business leaders, with feedback from these leaders on participant behavior and general interest. These tours involved some half-day job shadowing for participants to observe both what work was being done and how employees were getting the work done.

• At key points in the training, participants were placed into one or two weeks of full-time internship experience, involving on-the-job training with regular feedback on performance from the employers.

• When possible, MPTC employed a business employee to serve as a part-time trainer along with the college's trainer. This added constant reinforcement and application of classroom training to the real world. It also created an excellent private sector employment reference for the participants.

• Participants were provided daily feedback from the college trainer and peer participants on their soft skills. This feedback helped them see that breaking old habits takes time and continuous reinforcement.

• All training received college-transcripted credit. This created a permanent MPTC record for the participants and served as a recruiting tool for future education and upgrading of the participants.

• The college, employers, and social services emphasized career ladder opportunities for further education and advancement. Participants learned that the transcripted credits, along with the future life experiences to be gained through employment, presented them with opportunities for advanced placement into college programs.

- As participants completed their training experience, the college held graduation ceremonies to celebrate achievements. Friends, family, potential employers, the media, and faculty all attended this celebration, which helped make this training part of a positive transitioning experience from welfare to work.

Soft Skills

The MPTC mission statement references "building a competitive workforce" by preparing its students for the world of work. This involves teaching not only technical skills but also skills in attitudes and values that contribute to the student's success on entering the workplace. In 1988, area employers identified seven critical soft skills areas: work productively, work cooperatively, communicate clearly, learn effectively, act responsibly, value self positively, and think critically and creatively. If employers are asked why people get fired from their jobs, the answer usually involves an inability to cooperate and work well with others or act responsibly or a lack of adaptability. Clearly, a major element of success for many new employees rests with soft skills as well as the appropriate level of technical, or hard, skills.

This concept of soft skills was not new to MPTC, which had developed and delivered soft skill competency training as part of its credit-based courses since 1988. Until this welfare reform challenge, however, the college had not adequately addressed how it would adapt short-term training or individual noncredit courses to incorporate soft skills.

The college attempted to be responsive to the needs of employers and welfare recipients through this training, but how would the trainer know if changes in the level of soft skills had in fact occurred during this short period? The answer came in administering the video-based Workplace Success Skills assessment instrument both before and after the training. This instrument was (and is) used by employers nationwide to assess the employability skill levels of prospective and incumbent workers based on the Secretary's Commission on Achieving Necessary Skills. The assessment produced a detailed report on the broad skill areas of listening, interacting with others, organizing work, and learning skills. The pretraining assessment served to guide faculty in teaching specific competencies and modifying curriculum to individual student needs. The posttraining assessment report served to communicate soft skill proficiency to potential employers by serving as a supplemental transcript on soft skills. The report also served as a benchmark for employers if they chose to reassess these workers later to measure growth during employment. To funding agencies, MPTC could then document the value participants received (learning and growth) during training in an objective, quantifiable way. To area employers, the report indicated that the college was listening to their expressed concerns regarding soft skill training.

MPTC targeted the appropriate levels of soft skills in its WNW short-term training to be measured by the Workplace Success Skills assessments. The delivery of these soft skill applications was accomplished in a variety of ways:

- Delivering esteem-building workshops for participants
- Incorporating lessons from *The 7 Habits of Highly Effective People* (Covey, 1990) as a major training component.
- Providing instructor feedback on how each participant demonstrated soft skills during training
- Providing internship opportunities as part of the training program, with employer feedback on soft and hard skills demonstrated
- Using a pre- and posttraining assessment instrument to measure change in soft skills of participants
- Offering a supplemental twenty-four-hour job retention workshop

Conclusion

When unemployment rates are low, employers are forced to accept a lower level of job competencies (hard skills) required for entry-level employment. This is due to the smaller pool of workers and greater competition among employers, some of whom adopt the recruiting strategy of offering an additional ten cents per hour to attract new workers. When unemployment rates are high, higher levels of job competencies (hard skills) are required for entry-level employment. This is because the pool of workers is larger and there is less perceived competition among employers. The level of soft skills required, however, will remain a constant need. The cost of high turnover and lost productivity due to poor soft skills is much greater (in the short-term) than the risks associated with lower hard skills, which can be taught more easily on the job.

Partner agencies include the college and governmental organizations for social services and workforce development. The employer community consists of large and small employers, union and non-union shops, manufacturing and service sector employers, chambers of commerce, and urban and rural employers. WNW participants are students and their families and dependents.

It is understandable that there would be a wide range of interest and required change among these three primary groups. The key was whether the three could coordinate their changes so none of them created a situation where they would win and the others would lose. For example, meaningful welfare reform would not have occurred if the partner agencies were in total control and the employers and WNW participants perceived that they would lose as a result. It would not be effective if employers won but

WNW participants and partner agencies perceived loss. Were the three key players equally yoked and equally succeeding? Part of the answer was having clear communication, with a clear understanding of how each defined success and how the key players were interdependently moving toward their respective success indicators and a common vision.

Unfortunately, there was the perception that partner agencies had difficulty avoiding turf issues and pursuing a common agenda effectively. These working relationships among agencies continued to improve over time. Less visible in this change process, however, was the competition that occasionally occurred within the employer community and between WNW participants. This was where the employer community needed a champion to step forward to bring focus and light to the challenges of setting priorities and painting the bigger workforce picture. Similarly, the WNW participants needed a facilitator or leader to advocate for their needs in a proactive, coordinated manner. All three groups needed to be open to change, and over time, all needed to be driven more by the passion of what the community was doing rather than reacting out of fear over what the community was or was not doing. The critical lesson learned from these dynamics was that leadership was needed within and between these three major groups to refocus all parties on the higher community goal of economic development and individual self-sufficiency.

The community steering committee completed its two-year goal of reducing the AFDC caseload in Fond du Lac County, shared its successes and failures with other governmental units, provided input to the governor's office and legislators regarding W-2 legislation, and celebrated its efforts in a community luncheon with the governor. The members then identified three further areas for action:

Prevention. Early alert systems could be strengthened to keep individuals and families off welfare rolls. This would include a greater role by the public school systems.

Retention. Employers could address issues at the workplace that might result in improved retention rates. These would include training of frontline supervisors to serve a stronger coach and mentor role, as well as further soft skills training experiences for employees.

Promotion. Greater attention could be focused on ensuring that employees receive the opportunity to advance on the job by participating in further training (either on their own time or through company-sponsored training).

Has the welfare reform initiative worked in Wisconsin? Has it affected the technical colleges? The answer is yes on both counts, but with certain qualifiers.

Wisconsin's transition into W-2 has been well publicized and has resulted in tens of thousands of individuals moving from welfare to work.

The technical colleges, labor unions, employers, and partner agencies stressed the need to have coordinated training, though this proved to be a challenge. The driving force for change in W-2 continued to be work first. More recently, Wisconsin has elected to apply some TANF funds for a program entitled Workforce Attachment and Advancement. Ten million dollars has been allocated for the purpose of training and other support systems necessary to attract new workers and then retain incumbent workers qualifying for the funding (both employer-sponsored training and individual initiated training). The funds are allocated to Wisconsin's eleven Workforce Investment Boards for appropriation. There are several examples of technical colleges partnering with business clusters, as well as with quasi-public organizations to deliver pre- and postemployment training. This represents a major opportunity for college involvement. It also represents corrective legislation that many believe was overlooked in W-2.

The Wisconsin welfare reform experience is still unfolding, as it is in other states. State legislation must be coordinated with the federal Workforce Investment Act, the Welfare to Work Act, and many other complementary and sometimes conflicting laws. The task of educating and training Wisconsin's workforce has not diminished; rather, it has increased. The rules have changed, the technical colleges are now having to work in establishing new and changing partnerships, and the funding levels to accomplish this challenge are diminishing. As before under JTPA, the two-year colleges will find a way to remain a key player in building a competitive workforce.

Reference

Covey, S. R. *The 7 Habits of Highly Effective People: Powerful Lessons in Personal Change.* New York: Simon & Schuster, 1990.

DENNIS H. NITSCHKE was vice president of corporate and community services for Moraine Park Technical College from 1992 through 2000. He is currently president of his own consulting company, Landmark Opportunities, in Menasha, Wisconsin.

5

This chapter describes the program, administrative implications, and lessons learned from the Advanced Technology Program, a welfare-to-work program developed by Oakland Community College in Michigan, over the past six years.

The Advanced Technology Program: A Welfare-to-Work Success Story

Karen Pagenette, Cheryl Kozell

In 1995, Representative Hubert Price, Jr., convinced the Michigan State legislature to support a pilot project at Oakland Community College (OCC) to train welfare recipients in high-skill areas. OCC was chosen because of its experience working with high-risk populations using nontraditional training and delivery methods. The project was based on the following premises: (1) that welfare recipients require full-time employment in high-paying jobs to reach total self-sufficiency; (2) in order to obtain high-paying jobs, participants need skills training; (3) in order to remain and advance in their employment, participants require continuing education; and (4) the training has to meet the labor demand needs of the local economy in order to ensure jobs for graduates. The Advanced Technology Program is the result of this pilot project. The program is still being offered today to the working poor, who cannot expect to raise their standard of living and become self-sufficient without skills training.

Community colleges have long been known for their ability to serve a diverse student population. However, even OCC's extensive experience with nontraditional students and nontraditional instruction did not adequately prepare it to cope with the demands of the Advanced Technology Program. The participants in this program come from backgrounds fraught with crises, and any disruption in their day-to-day routine can cause them to abandon their training plans. The college's goal from the beginning of the Advanced Technology Program has been to try to remove any obstacle that interferes with training. It requires constant review, but the rewards of the program are well worth the effort. Describing the challenges of the program is easy; describing the benefits of the program is not. The data on program completion and job

NEW DIRECTIONS FOR COMMUNITY COLLEGES, no. 116, Winter 2001   © John Wiley, & Sons, Inc.

placement do not begin to describe the value of the program. It is only by see-
ing the joy and pride on the faces of the graduates and knowing the positive
impact the program has had on their families in breaking the cycle of welfare
that observers can begin to understand why it was so important for OCC to
develop this program and ensure its success.

Outcomes of the Advanced Technology Program

Since the program began in 1995, over 250 participants have been enrolled, 98 percent of them women. The average age of the participants is
twenty-nine, and none of them had previously completed a college degree,
although 62 percent had completed at least one postsecondary course or
vocational program. Through the spring of 2000, when a major change
was made in the delivery of training, group completion rates generally
exceeded 80 percent. For participants who completed training, placement
into full-time training-related jobs has consistently been around 90 percent. Approximately 85 percent of participants are reported to have their
cash assistance cases closed within one year of their placement date. The
average placement salary rate for successful completers is above $20,000,
with a range of $19,000 to $25,000, including comprehensive benefits.
Follow-up surveys of graduates of the program show an annual average
salary increase of $2,000. Some graduates of five and six years ago report
salaries in the $35,000 to $40,000 range.

Key Components of the Advanced Technology Program

The Advanced Technology Program has four key components: industry
partnerships, career opportunities, a community-based task force, and a
strong administrative support structure. These components are essential to
the success of welfare-to-work training programs. The absence of any one
of them would leave a void in the program that could not be carried solely
by the other components.

Industry Partnerships. One of the objectives of the program is that
the participants will gain full-time employment in high-paying jobs with
comprehensive benefits. In order to ensure that this objective is obtained,
OCC's goal is for employers to commit to hiring program graduates. Obtaining this commitment requires trust on the part of the employer that the participants who apply for employment will have the skills and ability to
perform the job in a dependable and efficient manner. Building this trust
requires that the employer have intimate knowledge of the content of the
training and confidence that participants have successfully gained the competencies targeted in the training.

OCC has been successful in building employer trust by engaging
employers in the curriculum development and training delivery process as

much as feasible. Once a company has been identified as having a need for skills in a particular occupational area that can be taught in six months or less, representatives of the companies are enlisted to meet with content experts from the college. This team then identifies training components, which can come from credit classes already established by the college or noncredit selections created specifically for the employer needs, to address the competencies needed for specific job classifications.

In addition to curriculum development involvement, company representatives are encouraged to come into the classroom to engage in activities with the participants, such as delivering information about their corporate culture or offering workshops on professional topics.

Another important role the employer plays to develop communication and trust with the college is to serve in an advisory capacity on the program task force. The company is usually represented by at least one person from the higher decision-making level of the company and, ideally, someone at the operational level.

The size and reputation of the companies involved in the project are very important to recruiting participants for the program. Welfare recipients are not interested in just any job; they are interested in a career with a company that is respected in the community and offers long-term employment opportunities. The risk of failure for this population is very high. The participants have to believe that the rewards at the end of the program will be worth the effort it will cost them to abandon welfare in favor of competing in the job market.

To date, industry partners in the Advanced Technology Program include EDS Corporation, Kelly Services, Deco Group, Xerox, and Fanuc Robotics. All of these corporate partners have been involved in developing curriculum, recruiting and selecting participants, developing a placement process, providing information about their corporate culture, promoting the program, and providing paid internships in some cases.

Career Opportunities. Providing an opportunity to build a career is a unique feature of the program. The intent of the program was not just to get people into jobs. In Michigan at the time the pilot project was proposed, placement into a job was the only option offered to welfare recipients; training was not an option. Until $100,000 was appropriated for the pilot project at OCC in 1995, funds were not made available for training. After two years of successful results with the Advanced Technology Program, the state allocated $12.5 million across the state for training.

In order to convince the state that training could contribute to personal self-sufficiency, the payoff for the expense of training needed to be the kind of results that would provide a person with opportunities to develop skills that could put him or her into jobs with opportunities to increase earning power over time. Advancement on the job generally requires continuing skill development through continuing education and training. For this reason, the training components of the program include college credit whenever possible so that these credits later can be applied toward a degree or certificate in a postsecondary program.

Many of the program graduates return to school once they establish themselves in a job. Most of the companies offer some tuition reimbursement. A scholarship fund has been established for the graduates to encourage their return to school.

Furthermore, career advising is included as a component of the program. Group sessions and one-on-one sessions are provided to the participants in which they receive assistance in making career decisions based on current labor market information and personal goals and interests.

A Community-Based Task Force. Having political support, such as Representative Price as a champion of the program, greatly facilitated the establishment of a community-based task force. The support of key players in the community is as important to a program like this as the jobs and content of the classes. The task force for the Advanced Technology Program includes local leaders, the local Workforce Development Board representatives, industry partners, Michigan Family Independence Agency (the state welfare agency), community-based organizations, the faith community, the Child Care Coordinating Agency, the Transit Authority, representatives of the state jobs commission, and welfare job club providers, as well as college staff. This group has been meeting regularly for over six years. Open communication on a regular basis in an environment where personal and political agendas are put aside has allowed college staff who are coordinating the program to move through bureaucratic layers that have the potential to impede participant success. Organizations represented through the task force have provided resources to the participants as needed and in a timely manner. Resources for transportation, child care, housing, medical care, personal counseling, and professional wardrobes have all been coordinated with the goals of the program in mind. It is essential that task force members be high enough administrators in their organization that they can influence appropriate action within the company or agency.

Administrative Support Structure. The Advanced Technology Program is very labor intensive, and costs more than traditional training programs. Even with collaborative agreements with social and community service agencies to provide support services, college staff have to provide not only training but case management services as well, which increases the cost of the program. In order to offer the Advanced Technology Program, OCC had to secure grant funds from both Michigan and the federal government. That meant that the program had to be in compliance with the requirements of both funding agencies. OCC has successfully operated the program under these restrictions from the beginning because the program director was experienced at managing grants from both funding sources simultaneously. Having someone with expertise in grant administration is one of the keys to the success of the Advanced Technology Program.

Another administrative challenge in funding the Advanced Technology Program is the costs that occur because of individual participants' life situations that interfere with training—for example, eviction notices, unresolved court judgments, and even lack of appropriate business attire. Usually, these costs cannot be supported with grant funds, so the college had to identify private funding sources to address these issues. The OCC Foundation was instrumental in securing private funds to establish an emergency fund for the Advanced Technology Program to address non-training-related expenses. Without those funds, several of the program participants would have dropped out. Using existing college fundraising resources to address unanticipated costs is another key to the success of the program.

The support of key leaders at the college was instrumental for the success of the Advanced Technology Program. These were not just leaders in the administrative ranks of the college. The program staff worked with functional leaders throughout the college in areas such as financial services, registration, and counseling in order to get changes made to the college's academic and support systems. Without a mandate from the leaders of the college to make the necessary changes and the cooperation of the functional leaders, Advanced Technology Program staff would either have been stopped from running the program effectively or would have been so mired down in administrative minutia that they could not have maintained the program's momentum. With the help of key leaders, many changes were made to the college's operating system that proved to be valuable and necessary. Changes such as an open entry–open exit instructional delivery system were introduced, changes were made in the college's pricing structure, and registration was handled differently for classes involving credit or noncredit options. Many of these changes affected college policies. With the support of the leadership, changing policy was quicker, easier, and sustainable.

The Training

Job-specific technical training is preceded by a job readiness component that corresponds to the technical area of study. This first component focuses on skills that employers have identified in such national surveys as the 1991 Secretary's Commission on Achieving Necessary Skills Report on common workplace skills. These are often referred to as soft skills and are addressed in classes on time management using personal calendars, goal setting, and governing values; problem solving and critical thinking; communication and conflict resolution; teamwork; and career development and employability skills (such as resumé writing and interviewing). Concepts such as teamwork and problem-solving techniques are integrated into all course work. Participants spend approximately 150 hours in these classes, which represent about a fourth of the total time in training.

Job-specific technical training is based on employer input. Through a job task analysis process, specific technical competencies are established. Existing college course work is used when appropriate, and new course work is developed as necessary. In the original format of the program, participants spent at least thirty hours a week in the technical training phase of the program, with the length of the technical training ranging between ten and fifteen weeks. As the program evolved over the years, this format was adjusted to meet the changing needs of welfare recipients.

The career opportunities for which training has been offered to participants in the program have included positions in the information technology industry such as systems administrator, software troubleshooting, COBOL programming, and business information systems. In the manufacturing area, positions such as robotic technicians and computer numerical control machinists were also options available.

Enhancements to the Program

Over the years that the program has been in operation, additional dimensions have enhanced the program's impact on the participants who have demonstrated their commitment to obtaining self-sufficiency.

Emergency Funding. The stress of unexpected expenses can deter anyone's focus on tasks such as skill attainment. Starting in the second year, private donors gave more than $20,000 to be used for support services for emergencies such as court fees, medical and dental expenses, and car repairs not allowed by other public sources. These funds have been replenished through private fundraising done by the OCC Foundation and used throughout the remaining program years.

Support After Training. United Way of Oakland awarded the program $25,000 to be used for support services needed after training was completed while the program participants were trying to establish self-sufficiency. For example, child care costs, family medical care, and support for continuing education were provided to graduates who obtained training-related employment and continued to show progress on the job. These funds were used to aid in job retention. A condition for requesting this resource was the requirement that the graduate submit evidence of personal budget management efforts and proof of need.

Individual Development Accounts. Approximately $15,000 of the United Way award was used for requests for unexpected expenses after placement. The remaining $10,000 was used to establish a matching fund for the creation of individual development accounts for which eligible graduates could put earned income into a savings account, to be matched dollar for dollar by federal funds. The purpose of the account is to save for a down payment on a house or pay for education. Ten graduates have elected to participate in this opportunity. Thus far, one graduate has been able to save enough money to purchase her own home. Six of the remaining nine are still on schedule for their savings plan.

The college partnered with a community-based organization that managed the administration of the funds in order to provide this opportunity to successful program participants. Students who retained their employment with their original employer after training are eligible to apply for these funds. Applicants are screened for efforts to clear their credit records and potential to maintain a savings account. They also attend financial counseling workshops as part of the program. Applicants who are not selected to participate also receive counseling advice on clearing up credit records.

Flexible Training Options. In addition to enhancements to the program for the benefit of the personal circumstances of the participants, changes have been made to the format of the program to address the changing needs of the working poor.

As welfare reform has moved more people off cash assistance and into employment, the numbers of working poor, who still have to depend on some level of public assistance, have increased. At the same time, those who have remained on cash assistance are in greater need of basic workplace skills.

The original format for delivering training was designed to reflect a schedule of a typical professional work environment as much as possible, with a cohort of participants attending the same classes together, Monday through Friday, from 9:00 A.M. to 3:30 P.M. This schedule was also designed to leave adequate time for the required part-time employment (twenty to thirty hours per week.)

Beginning in February 2000, the training program was modified considerably to offer a more flexible self-paced, open entrance–open exit format to accommodate heavier working schedules. It also allows for more customization of skill attainment and accommodation for different achievement levels.

Under this new format, participants started with a block of five weeks of classes where they all met together in one group from 9:00 A.M. to 12:00 P.M. for their soft skill classes. The occupational and technical skills training could be accessed based on their individual availability from 8:00 A.M. to 8:00 P.M., Monday through Friday, plus Saturday hours, in a learning lab setting covered by an instructor who functions more as a facilitator than a lecturer. After the initial five weeks, the training schedule was almost entirely self-paced, with the exception of six hours a week when the students met in classes for additional soft skills training.

In addition, training is now competency based. That is, it is divided into modules targeting specific and discrete competencies. Participants move to advanced levels only after demonstrating successful mastery of each competency. This model may result in some participants' completing training in less than six months and others extending their training schedule beyond six months.

Lessons Learned

Six years of delivering the Advanced Technology Program and the evaluation of the various configurations of the training model have provided many lessons for future offerings of the program.

Need for Structure. The move to a self-paced model requires personal discipline to maintain adequate progress through the assigned modules. The content of the personal time management class was modified to address the special considerations for participating in a less structured and self-paced environment. The participants were required to develop and submit a schedule that addressed training, work, and personal responsibilities. Nevertheless, program staff began to see retention in the training program plummet to below 50 percent.

It appeared that the change in the structure of the training schedule had a negative impact on the high retention rates that were experienced in the first five years of operating the program. Although no scientific measurement was applied to prove this causation, it is reasonable to assume that this change did have some impact on the retention rate that for close to five years was significantly different.

There was, however, also a decline in the retention rate for the year just prior to the application of the self-paced format. Program managers have attributed this to two other changes in the welfare arena. The first was the progress that was made in moving welfare recipients off cash assistance, leaving the individuals who had lower basic workplace skills in the recruitment pool for the program. Also, the personal barriers are greater for this current pool. Despite support services available to address many barriers, some of the participants leave training when they become overwhelmed.

The second factor that occurred at the same time that the program delivery structure changed was that federal welfare laws changed. New instructions for training options were applied for cash recipients only. A person on cash assistance was now allowed to participate in a thirty-hour a week training program of six months or less duration without having to meet the thirty-hours a week work requirement mandated by earlier legislation. For some people, this allowed them to choose training instead of working without a real commitment to the learning process. This lack of commitment led to more than the usual number of participants who either failed to maintain a consistent attendance pattern or over time lost interest in completing the training.

This drastic reduction in retention rate caused the college to rethink the program's self-paced format. What has resulted is a hybrid version of the earlier open entrance–open exit format that now also includes a self-paced basic skills-building lab.

Several features were added to the program design to address issues that appeared to be affecting student success:

Students are enrolled longer in the scheduled group-size activities at the start of their training plan in order for them to demonstrate the self-discipline that is necessary for the self-paced format of the technical training.

More options are built into the program that allow students to exit at points in the technical skills training as a completer of a specific set of skills that can be used in a specific job. Options for reentering are also more flexible with this new structure.

The need for appropriate communication as well as technical skills has been recognized and addressed. In order to complete a phase of training, students must demonstrate competence not only in technical training but also in the communication skills established for each phase.

The group meeting for case management was eliminated, and a requirement that each student must make a weekly appointment with the program case manager to discuss progress in the program and associated personal issues was added.

Advantages for Combining Work with School. Experience has shown that the students who work at least some minimal number of hours during training demonstrate a greater capacity to stay focused and disciplined in completing their training. The ideal design would be a program that incorporates a part-time work schedule that alternates with, as well as accommodates, the classroom training schedule. This design is the preferred choice of arrangement to negotiate with potential corporate partners.

Foundational Skill Building. Foundational and basic skills are a particular challenge with the new pool of program candidates. In order to give a wider range of welfare recipients the opportunity to participate in a program such as the Advanced Technology Program, the college has sought additional funding to develop a self-paced basic skills learning environment. This year, funds have been secured to make a laboratory for this purpose a reality. The college is now able to offer a user-friendly option for building basic workplace skills. The design of the model is such that the basic skill building is presented as another extension of the technical skills training. This type of learning environment has worked well for all participants in the program due to the user-friendly technology in use, immediate and continuous feedback provided to the students, and the personal interaction between students and instructors.

Employer Influence on Recruitment. The influence that a corporate partner can have on recruitment cannot be overemphasized. The visible presence of an employer during recruitment activities and involvement in the screening process are effective strategies for recruiting interested candidates for training. An employer stressing the importance of training and supporting a specific training option goes a lot further than any college recruiter in getting the kinds of results needed to fill classes and laboratories.

As more employers became interested in interviewing graduates of the program, the tendency of program staff was to do less promotion of a specific employer. Initial corporate partners also found it harder as time went on to maintain staff who could participate in these kinds of activities. These tendencies had a negative impact on recruitment.

The lesson to be learned for employer involvement is that the corporate presence is significant for recruitment and that it is important not to depend too heavily upon a specific employer. Things change for them in their own corporate climate, and it is necessary to be sensitive to their needs as well. Although they may not be able to maintain a consistent level of involvement over long periods of time, giving them a break by widening the pool of employer partners will allow them to stay involved but not necessarily carry the full load. For this reason, getting involved with a professional organization may result in the capacity to keep a flow of interested employers participating at the level necessary to impact recruitment levels.

Mentoring: Benefits and Challenges. Corporate partners have developed mentoring structures within their corporate climate to address the needs of the graduates of the program, who generally do not have much professional experience in the corporate world. This has been reported to be very effective by both participants and employers in terms of improving employment retention. For the same reasons that corporate participation in recruitment can be a challenge for the employer over time, sustaining mentoring programs throughout personnel changes and cutbacks can be a problem. The mentoring program requires that the supervisor assigned to the program graduate set aside time to be trained in the concept and philosophy of the program, establish and maintain a communication process with the graduate to provide advice and feedback, and help the graduate develop a career development plan. The program staff working with the community task force is exploring other resources within the college community and its external community to seek out mentoring options to assist corporate partners.

Conclusion

Colleges that are considering starting a welfare-to-work program should keep a few key concepts in mind to ensure the success of their program:

Implementing a successful welfare-to-work training program is a community endeavor. It takes the collaborative commitment of education, business and industry, community groups, social service agencies, and the participants themselves to deal with the training issues and life circumstances that impede training.

A successful welfare-to-work program focuses on career development, not just job placement. The program should provide long-term opportunities for participants to continue their education and advance in their professions.

A successful welfare-to-work program provides relevant technical and foundational skills training that meets the needs of the local economy.

Business partners participating in a successful welfare-to-work program should be well known and well respected in the community and show evidence of financial stability and growth over the long term.

A successful welfare-to-work program will challenge the existing administrative structure of the community college as it forces the institution to find innovative ways to serve a high-risk population.

In a successful welfare-to-work program, the retention and promotion rates of the graduates will be as important as their training completion and job placement rates. It is through these measures—the real proof of program success—that a permanent break in the cycle of poverty for participants and their families can be demonstrated.

The OCC program has been recognized as an exemplary welfare-to-work program by many organizations and institutions, including the American Association of Community College, the U.S. Department of Labor, and the National Association of Continuing Education and Training.

Reference

The Secretary's Commission on Achieving Necessary Skills. "What Work Requires of Schools: A SCANS Report for America 2000." Washington, D.C.: U.S. Department of Labor, June 1991.

KAREN PAGENETTE is director of the Career Development Unit of Workforce Development Services at Oakland Community College.

CHERYL KOZELL is executive director of advancement at Oakland Community College.

6

The development and implementation of a call center training program, to include the training of welfare recipients, is the focus of this chapter. Components of this program and its effects on both the consumer and corporate community are discussed.

Welfare to Work: Solutions or Snake Oil?

John W. Ream, Brenda G. Wagner, Robin C. Knorr

A few years ago, Kansas City, Missouri, and the surrounding communities found themselves in a predicament: the face of the community workforce had changed. The new face was that of a customer service representative (CSR), and local businesses needed many of them. The Metropolitan Community Colleges' Business and Technology Center (BTC) heard about the need, thought of a plan to fulfill the need, and has implemented a program that successfully meets the need.

Development of the BTC to Meet Community Needs

Fundamentally, there are significant barrier issues to providing welfare-to-work programs: welfare recipients have few skills, little work experience, poor soft skills, limited education, low-level basic skills, no support systems, and motivation and attitude issues, and they are typically stuck in a welfare culture. Nevertheless, the goal is for these individuals to become self-sufficient. An important milestone in this goal is not just getting a job but keeping it. Retention is the benchmark. If a welfare-to-work program is not retaining participants in work, then it is probably just snake oil.

In 1994, in response to Kansas City's Smart Cities campaign, the Metropolitan Community Colleges (MCC) expanded its role in the economic development of the greater Kansas City area. This campaign brought MCC in closer collaboration with the development leaders of the community, particularly the Kansas City Area Development Council (KCADC), who have supported the development of programs that ensure skilled workers are available and ready

NEW DIRECTIONS FOR COMMUNITY COLLEGES, no. 116, Winter 2001   © John Wiley, & Sons, Inc.

in the labor pool. The development of the BTC has been an important link in these collaborative efforts.

The BTC is the economic and workforce development arm of MCC that provides consulting, development, and training to Kansas City area businesses and organizations. The BTC operates from revenues generated by client contracts, without the benefit of state aid. The BTC has over 120 client accounts with multiple projects serviced by a staff of ninety professionals. Sixty-five percent of the work is conducted at clients' business sites by full-time performance consultants. The BTC was the incubator from which the Call Center Training Program was born and developed.

Kansas City is a primary location for call centers in the central United States. The greater Kansas City bistate area has more than twenty-five major inbound call center companies. There are over forty thousand CSR job positions, with approximately three hundred job openings occurring every month. The average turnover rate for these positions is 35 percent. And it costs employers at least $7,000 and as much as $16,000 to recruit and train each new CSR employee (Burch and Mann, 1998). Kansas City continues to attract new companies, and existing companies often relocate their call center operations there.

The Kansas City area has a tight labor market, an unemployment rate of 2.8 percent, and a shortage of skilled workers (Burch and Mann, 1998). The need for skilled CSRs is especially acute; it is so strong, in fact, that companies often compete for workers. The logical solution is to develop a CSR workforce by tapping populations that are not working and train them with the skills to meet this need. Although there have been layoffs for CSR workers, these individuals are typically absorbed quickly by local or regional employers, depending on their skill level.

Among the various populations in the Kansas City area are a large number of welfare recipients who currently are not employed. In Jackson County alone, as of April 2001, there were 8,045 families on the welfare rolls (Jackson County Division of Family Services, 2001). In addition, there are dislocated workers from companies that are downsizing, educationally and economically disadvantaged individuals, and others in need of job skills training. The BTC knew these individuals could be trained as CSRs and placed in jobs that paid well above minimum wage, provided individual and family benefits, and offered multiple opportunities for personal and career growth.

The Initial Process

In the fall of 1995, the BTC sponsored a forum for companies with major call centers in Kansas City. Building a successful training program meant starting from where the jobs are and building the program to meet employer needs. In order to make that program successful for welfare recipients—by addressing employability, attitudes, and communication skills—one needs to go well beyond job demand and make sure the design incorporates components that many traditional programs often ignore.

The BTC conducted a needs assessment and found that the employer demand for skilled CSRs was quite high, as was turnover; employers were looking to the BTC for resources. The dialogue eventually led to a proposed call center training facility to be located at the BTC. The concept was that employers would provide good job opportunities, the BTC would design and conduct the training program, and the community-based agencies would provide participants and training funds from their entitlement programs. This concept was the seed for the development of a self-sustaining call center training operation that would provide jobs for economically and educationally disadvantaged individuals. It required the businesses to make the first commitment before others could follow.

AT&T and Lucent Technologies responded first with a contribution of telephone equipment for the proposed sixty-four-station state-of-the-art call center training facility. Gateway followed with top-of-the-line computer equipment, and Sprint, DST, and Citibank made cash donations. The Missouri Department of Workforce Development and the Missouri Department of Elementary and Secondary Education provided additional funding for completion of the 5,000-square-foot facility designed and configured by call center industry experts. These companies became the core business partners. BTC conducted on-site job and task analyses with partner companies to design curriculum and set benchmarks for assessments.

BTC and its business partners looked to the community-based agencies and their entitlement programs for participants and training funds. The Full Employment Council (the administrative entity for the local Small Business Administration) provided training funds for Temporary Assistance to Needy Families (TANF), formerly known as the Job Training Partnership Act (JTPA), and for welfare participants. The Missouri Department of Elementary and Secondary Education funded assessments through a contract agreement with the Division of Family Services. Project Refocus, a vocational rehabilitation and dislocated worker program, sent its program participants to the BTC and paid for their training. Across the state line, the Kansas Private Industry Council sent its JTPA-funded participants. These community-based organizations became BTC's primary agency partners.

Another major community partner, the Ewing Marion Kauffman Foundation, nationally known and recognized for its work in youth development and entrepreneurial leadership, donated $300,000 to develop the Supported Work Center, an important component in call center training.

To remain competitive in the marketplace, the business partners needed skilled, productive workers with specific competencies who were able to become permanent employees. The agency partners needed access to jobs with good wages, benefits, and career development so their program participants could be retained in the workplace. Agency partners needed educational institutions like the BTC to develop performance-based training programs to ensure that program participants learn the competencies that employers require. In turn, the BTC needed well-matched candidates for its Call Center Training Program and work placement. It looked to entitlement programs for these individuals and the funds to pay for the training. From its business partners, the BTC needed to be assured that graduates of the program placed into employment had adequate supervision, critical evaluations, and feedback systems in place for them to be retained.

The Program

The Call Center Training Program was designed to assist welfare recipients overcome the countless hurdles facing them in the workplace. Coordinators who joined the BTC Call Center team after having positions in private sector call centers taught the program.

The BTC Call Center. The BTC Call Center labs and workstations are patterned after professional CSR centers. Nonwelfare students are also enrolled in the training classes, giving each class a beneficial blend of life and work experiences.

The BTC Call Center Training Program extends over six weeks. Although this is an intense few weeks for participants and staff alike, the short time frame enables participants to complete their training before obstacles to that completion arise. Participants must have a high school diploma or general educational development (GED), reliable transportation, and no felony record, and they must sign a contract agreeing to dismissal from the program after a third absence. The referring agency, Missouri's Division of Family Services Futures Program, provides funding for child care for the duration of the program and until graduates are placed in jobs. Bus transportation has also been improved between area city centers and the BTC.

The Curriculum. In developing the curriculum, the BTC coordinators interviewed and observed CSR employees and their managers at Gateway, AT&T, GE Capital, and Citicorp. From this extensive job and task analysis, they identified the academic and specialized skills, aptitudes, and attitudes of successful workers. They then developed a curriculum that addresses these skills, as well as the multitasking these jobs require (for example, communicating with others, processing information, and solving problems, all while using sophisticated computer and telecommunications systems). Participants master the skills necessary to operate networked computers and telecommunications systems through hands-on practice at their own workstations. They learn basic principles of customer service theory and practices through lecture and demonstration, group discussion, textbook review, videos, and role playing using the center's Web-based simulated company applications. They build speed, efficiency, and poise while handling and processing customer inquiries, requests, and complaints through "live" calls to one another and, ultimately, to and from the public.

The BTC places a major emphasis on learning acceptable and expected workplace behavior and teamwork—skills that participants might not need to land a job but will definitely need to keep one. Students also practice communicating effectively and professionally using appropriate vocabulary, tone, timing, and enunciation. Mastering all of these components and learning a professional dress code and the importance of a strong teamwork attitude make for an individual who is suited for success.

Part of the curriculum includes requiring students to identify and record short-term and long-term professional and personal goals, thereby enabling them to determine which goals require additional education and training. Among other activities included in the program, students learn to prepare resumés, participate in intense, antagonistic job interviews, use the Internet and other resources to research potential employers, and write cover letters for their resumés and, subsequently, thank-you notes to send following an interview. All of this and more prepare students for what lies ahead: placement in a company.

Life After the Program. The placement and tracking components of the BTC's Call Center Training Program provide participants with opportunities to assess multiple employment options. Area call center employers and representatives make hour-long presentations about their companies and cover issues such as current job openings, wages, benefits, and career growth opportunities. Once a student is interested in a particular company and that company appears to be able to meet his or her professional and personal needs, students share their prepared resumés with the representative in an effort to arrange an interview. Although it is very common for program graduates to find a job this way, others find a job on their own using the job search skills they learned in class. On a rare occasion, students find that being a CSR is not for them; the call center staff then works closely with that individual to identify jobs for which his or her aptitudes and new skills are readily transferable. Graduate follow-up is conducted by telephone and by mail surveys every thirty, sixty, and ninety days following graduation. On occasion, visits to the workplace by instructors where graduates have accepted a position are also made.

The Results. Since January 1997, 541 participants have enrolled in the program, with 496 (92 percent) completing the course. Of the 496 students who completed the program, 362 (73 percent) obtained employment. Of the students who became employed, 85 percent remained on their job for at least ninety days. The range of pay has been from $7 per hour to more than $15 per hour. The average pay for program graduates is typically between $9 and $11 per hour.

The BTC engages in follow-up procedures that include some monitoring of the graduate's progress on their new job. The BTC conducts a paper or telephone survey with the employer when the student completes the employer's in-house training and when the student has completed ninety days on the job. This information has helped BTC to determine the effectiveness of its assessment techniques.

Looking Ahead

The Call Center Training Program at the BTC has become well known. Among other awards, the training program was the recipient of the 1999 American Association of Community Colleges/U.S. Department of Labor Workforce Development Award and the Vision 2000 Model of Excellence Award for Call Center Training. The BTC Call Center has been featured in several newspapers, publications, and television news reports throughout the Midwest as well.

In an effort to showcase the complete facility to potential CSRs, the BTC has held open house events, receptions, tours, and breakfasts for the work development agencies in the Kansas City area. The BTC also conducts a direct mail campaign specifically for the call center that is targeted to high school groups, working adults, and welfare agencies. In 1999, a call center start-up package was developed with other community colleges in mind. The package now includes a sales video, CDs, program implementation guides, and hands-on assistance from the BTC, and has been sold to other colleges and organizations across the country and overseas. These key marketing events and efforts continue to be well attended and received. Classes typically reach full capacity. The BTC Call Center continues to grow and provide services and opportunities for other community colleges and its corporate market.

References

Burch, W., and Mann, B. *Workforce Skills and Assessment Job Analysis*. Unpublished study. Kansas City, Mo.: Business & Technology Center, Metropolitan Community Colleges, 1998.

Jackson County Division of Family Services. *Monthly Management Report*. Kansas City, Mo.: Jackson County Division of Family Services, 2001.

JOHN W. REAM *is associate director of training and development at the Metropolitan Community College Business and Technology Center in Kansas City, Missouri.*

BRENDA G. WAGNER *is call center manager at the Metropolitan Community College Business and Technology Center in Kansas City, Missouri.*

ROBIN C. KNORR *is marketing manager at the Metropolitan Community College Business and Technology Center in Kansas City, Missouri.*

7

This chapter discusses postsecondary training programs and services for welfare recipients at a Colorado community college.

The Importance of Postsecondary Training for Welfare to Work: Initiatives at the Community College of Aurora

Daniela Higgins

To compete in today's employment market, it is evident that individuals benefit greatly from college training. Education is a means to economic independence and social mobility in the United States, and college training is increasingly important in reaching long-term economic stability. The average person who attends a two-year community college earns about 10 percent more than those without any college education, even without completing an associate degree (Kane and Rouse, 1995). Average expected lifetime earnings for a graduate with an associate degree are about $250,000 more than for an individual with only a high school diploma (Phillippe, 2000). A 2000 job survey of the metropolitan Denver area reveals that the average pay for jobs requiring high school completion but no experience or training was $9.62. An associate degree or certification raised the average wage to $14.47. For those with a bachelor's degree, the wage increased to $21.09. Jobs that required an advanced degree paid $24.62 an hour, or $51,209 annually (Colorado Department of Labor and Employment, 2001).

Because many jobs require college training, Temporary Aid for Needy Families (TANF) recipients who have access to job training through postsecondary education have a higher chance of achieving financial independence. A 1997 survey of 569 Aid to Family with Dependent Children (AFDC) recipients in Maine found, from 352 responses, that those who attended college experienced higher employment rates and earnings than those without college (Seguino and Butler, 1998). Gittell, Schehl, and Facri (1990) conducted a nine-year follow-up study of 158 women who received public assistance when they enrolled in New York colleges in 1980 and who then received either a two-year or four-year degree. Eighty-seven percent of the women left welfare after graduation, 89 percent had been employed since graduation, and almost half of the respondents were earning more than $20,000 per year at the time of the study in 1980. In addition to the economic benefits of graduation, the women reported improved lifestyles, better standards of living, and greater self-esteem. Among families headed by African American women, the poverty rate declines from 51 percent to 21 percent with at least one year of postsecondary education (Sherman, 1990).

For welfare recipients to move beyond the grasp of welfare poverty or being the working poor, an education that prepares them for higher-wage jobs is a huge benefit. Although postsecondary education may not be suitable for all TANF recipients, those who are interested should be encouraged and supported through the community college.

Initiatives at the Community College of Aurora Center for Workforce Development

For over a decade, the Community College of Aurora (CCA) in Colorado has helped change the lives of welfare recipients and single parents through its Center for Workplace Development (CWD). In return, the program has helped the community grow stronger, producing competent individuals who are reentering the workplace. The program provides college credit job training, case management, job counseling, and job placement services to individuals in the metropolitan Denver area. The program works with local one-stop agencies, social services, nonprofit organizations, and companies for job placement.

Studies indicate that welfare recipients are most likely to achieve financial independence by earning a college degree. However, with the passage of welfare legislation in 1996, the Personal Responsibility and Work Opportunity Reconciliation Act (PRWORA), only short-term training that leads directly to a job, and not a college degree, counts as an allowable work activity.

TANF Services and Initiatives. Colorado supports the work-first philosophy. However, some counties are diligent in providing opportunities for TANF recipients to pursue higher education and job training. For instance, the Adams County Department of Social Services (ACDSS) contracts with the Community College of Aurora (CCA) to provide job readiness, academic training, and case management for TANF recipients.

The ACDSS pays 100 percent of college tuition and fees, books, supplies, transportation, and child care and provides a clothing allowance for individuals to attend classes and job training. Recipients are entitled to support services while in preemployment training and can use the funds to pay for such expenses as housing emergencies, car repairs, and household bills. Once they secure full-time employment, their cases are transferred to Goodwill Industries' Job Success Program, another contractor of ACDSS. The Goodwill program tracks and monitors for two years former TANF recipients who are now gainfully employed. While enrolled in the Goodwill program, participants qualify for additional support services funds, which they can use to further their education and training. ACDSS has one of the most innovative TANF plans in the metropolitan Denver area. The county's objective is to remove all possible obstacles that may preclude participant involvement in training, education, and employment. ACDSS encourages its contractors to create customized incentive plans for participants. On successful completion of the CCA internship program, participants also receive a monetary incentive that they can spend as they like.

Contracted Services. The ACDSS program provides a seven-week Essential Skills Certificate Workplace certificate for sixteen college credits, offered Monday through Friday, from 8 A.M. to 5 P.M. For individuals who do not have general educational development (GED), remediation classes are provided. The county supports three months of participation in GED classes. CCA partners with Aurora Public Schools (APS) for GED training materials. On completion of their GED, students are matriculated into the seven-week job readiness track. Students learn keyboarding skills; Windows, Word, and Excel software applications; customer service; problem solving; listening at work; and decision making. They also participate in job preparatory training and job search workshops. As an extension of the academic track, students can participate in an internship at a company site for two and a half weeks. They must work sixty hours at a company of their choice. On completion of the internship, they receive two college credits. The internship exposes them to the world of work and gives them hands-on job skills. Companies get the chance to preview the students for further job consideration. On graduation, students work with an employment counselor until they secure permanent employment. Students are trained in areas of finding and keeping a job, and they are taught coping skills and given advice on overcoming personal barriers.

TANF recipients attending CCA are also introduced to community involvement programs and projects. The purpose of this involvement is to acquaint them with community needs, relate classroom information to practical experiences, and understand the importance of community work. The service-learning program at the college collaborates with local programs and agencies within Aurora for student volunteer opportunities. CCA, with the assistance of ACDSS, provides monetary incentives for TANF students involved in community service. For some projects, students can bring their children, who can also participate and learn.

CCA has also started a family literacy program for TANF students and their children. The service-learning program at the college and some of the

AmeriCorps. students assist with the development of reading plans, help coordinate monthly reading workshops, and teach reading techniques to participants in order to enhance their children's reading interest and abilities.

CCA is developing a peer mentoring program to assist TANF students with academic needs, career guidance, tutoring, family support, and other areas. The service-learning students, CCA faculty, and CCA staff will be recruited and trained to participate in this program.

CCA also cultivates relationships with TANF students and their children. Family barbecues, holiday festivities, lunches, picnics, and other get-togethers build stronger relationships with staff, faculty, students, and their families. On completion of the CCA Essential Skills Certificate program, students can participate in the annual CCA graduation ceremonies. Family, friends, faculty members, and staff are all invited to celebrate this special occasion. With the help of ACDSS, TANF students are given monetary incentives for perfect attendance, passing their GED test, good grades, graduation, employment, and other accomplishments.

When TANF recipients secure full-time employment and are no longer receiving cash assistance, they are eligible for financial assistance to pursue higher education. Post-TANF recipients are strongly encouraged to further their studies for increased marketability. Financial assistance for this endeavor is available through the college and the Goodwill program.

CCA's Accomplishments. In 2000–2001, CCA served over 115 TANF recipients, placed over 55 individuals in full-time employment at an average hourly wage of $7.95, and ranked first out of twenty-seven contractors in Adams County for exceeding job placement goals and federal work participation rate goals. As a result, CCA was the only contractor to receive a $46,000 bonus from ACDSS. The college plans on developing a scholarship program with the bonus award funds for individuals who do not qualify for subsidized training dollars. In 1998, CCA served sixty TANF recipients. Fifty of these clients successfully completed their training, and forty-five were placed in jobs at an average annual salary of $19,000. This salary reflects a 243 percent increase in earnings compared to the welfare benefits a mother of two would receive yearly. Employment follow-up records indicate that forty of the forty-five individuals are still employed and are no longer receiving welfare benefits. As of July 1999, twenty-five TANF graduates from CCA's job training program found full-time unsubsidized employment. These cases were all transferred to Goodwill—Job Success Program. To date, twenty individuals are still working at an average annual salary of $18,500. All twenty women have moved off cash assistance. They are all still eligible for continued financial support and low-income child care from ACDSS.

Arapahoe/Douglas's One-Stop Career Center. Arapahoe/Douglas's One-Stop Career Center also provides training and education to the TANF population. This county's training programs are more open-ended, allowing the county to make a determination of training time on a case-per-case basis. Clients can select whatever training program interests them and have up to six months to pursue and graduate from a program. The program pays 100 percent of clients' training expenses and also provides child care, transportation, supplies, and books. Once a client graduates, that person must seek full-time employment. Clients also receive case management, job placement, and counseling services.

Success Stories

Janet, age thirty-four, a single mother of four girls, has been on and off welfare for over fourteen years. She was referred to CCA by Adams County Social Services. Janet met with a case manager and was immediately enrolled in the customer/computer training program at the college. She successfully completed all her classes and graduated from the program with excellent grades and was placed in job search; however, she struggled finding employment because her work experience was limited. Her case manager suggested an internship program to enrich Janet's work experience. Community work experience and internships are valuable and sometimes essential for participants in order to secure gainful employment. Her case manager found an internship site for Janet at the CCA's human resources (HR) department. Janet interned for about a month, performing various office tasks, and using her bilingual skills in English and Spanish. On completion of her internship, Janet was offered a paid part-time position in the HR department. Once on the job, she performed so well that her supervisor offered her a full-time position with benefits. Janet has been working in the HR department for over a year and a half and is now an employee with the State of Colorado. Janet stated the program helped her build her self-esteem and provided her with computer skills. She enjoys her job and is happy to be off the welfare rolls. She plans on furthering her education at the college in the near future.

Amy, age twenty, a single mother of a baby boy, also attended CCA's job training program. She faced welfare limitations but used her time wisely by participating in a short-term computer training program. Today, Amy works as an office manager in a computer company and is no longer on public assistance.

Conclusion

Once welfare recipients earn a college degree and have job training, they earn a sufficiently high wage to make many of them financially independent and no longer in need of public assistance. The Center for Workforce Development Program at the Community College of Aurora has attempted to develop a comprehensive welfare-to-work program that provides support services to enable individuals to get a job and includes job training for college credit that provides clients with job skills within a culture that fosters an appreciation for education as a mechanism for career advancement.

In order to serve the low-income population better, policymakers should expand access to postsecondary education and job training for welfare recipients and expand TANF-allowable work requirements so people can leave the welfare rolls and secure jobs that pay a living wage. Here are several recommendations for policymakers to help meet these goals:

- Extend educational opportunities to postsecondary institutions.
- Allow college and work-study programs to satisfy the work requirements.
- Establish a mentor program at community colleges to help women acclimate to college life, develop study skills, and plan for careers.
- Increase county and state contracts with postsecondary institutions to provide welfare recipients with job-specific training.
- Continue subsidy provisions of child care, transportation, support services, and job training.
- Continue to provide postemployment support groups and family life classes for welfare recipients that focus on stress reduction, time management, personal budgeting, and counseling, mentoring, and peer group support.

References

Colorado Department of Labor and Employment, Labor Market Information, Workforce Research and Analysis. *Denver Metro Job Vacancy Survey.* Denver: Colorado Department of Labor and Employment, May 2001.

Gittell, M., Schehl, M., and Facri, C. *From Welfare to Independence: The College Option.* New York: Ford Foundation, 1990.

Kane, T. J., and Rouse, C. E. "Labor Market Returns to Two- and Four-Year Colleges." *American Economic Review*, 1995, 600–614.

Phillippe, K. A. (ed.) *National Profile of Community Colleges*: Trends & Statistics (3rd ed.). Washington, D.C.:Community College Press, 2000.

Seguino, S., and Butler, S. *Struggling to Make Ends Meet in the Maine Economy: A Study of Former and Current AFDC/TANF Recipients.* Augusta, Me.: Maine Center for Economic Policy, 1998.

Sherman, A. *College Access and the JOBS Program.* Washington, D.C.: Center for Law and Social Policy, 1990.

DANIELA HIGGINS is director of the Center for Workforce Development and teaches classes in essential skills at the Community College of Aurora.

8

This chapter discusses how El Paso Community College linked welfare-to-work participants to college credit programs that offer realistic pathways to certificates, associate degrees, and bachelor degrees.

Moving Welfare Families into Economic Self-Sufficiency: A Model from El Paso Community College

Kathleen Bombach

The passage of the Personal Responsibility and Work Opportunity Reconciliation Act (PRWORA) in 1996 was heralded as an end to welfare as we know it. Originally conceived as a needed support so widows could stay at home raising their children, welfare by the 1960s had become a perceived social problem, blamed for the dissolution of the black family and the creation of an underclass of irresponsible fathers, sexually dissolute mothers, and illegitimate and neglected children. PRWORA ended welfare's status as an entitlement program for single parents and the few two-parent households that qualified. Now welfare recipients would be forced into the workforce at whatever wages they could command, even if those wages left the family worse off than they were before.

PRWORA's 1996 changes for welfare recipients were dramatic. No longer would welfare be an entitlement program for a single parent so that she might stay home and raise her children. Now she would be expected to spend her days looking for work until she found a job. Instead of attending classes, searching for work, or engaging in public service twenty hours a week, she would now be expected to engage in work search for thirty to thirty-five hours a week in two-parent families.

For community colleges, these changes signaled a rejection of education as the route out of poverty and dependency. Indeed, the human capital development approach, which is based on the idea that welfare recipients will prosper in the long run if they pursue the education they missed first, including literacy, English as a Second Language, general educational development (GED), and occupational training, has fallen out of favor. The new approach, labor force attachment, emphasizes immediate job search until a job, any job, is acquired. The belief behind a labor force attachment model is that it is the act of working that is instructive. Education is something that a recipient can always pursue later, on her own time.

Texas Initiatives for Welfare

In anticipation of the passage of the CAREERS Act in 1998 (which did not pass Congress), the Texas legislature passed House Bill 1863 and began reorganizing the state workforce development system. The legislature also created several state programs that existed outside the Job Training Partnership Act (JTPA) private industry council (PIC) and later Workforce Investment Act local workforce board structures. One of these programs was the Texas Self Sufficiency Fund (SSF). Under the SSF, public educational institutions and community-based organizations, along with at least one private sector employer, could form partnerships to train and prepare welfare recipients for jobs with the partner businesses. This program was completely independent of the federal welfare and workforce development dollars funneled through the state. Amid the confusion of new legislation, reorganization at the state and local levels, state-imposed provider contracts, and staff and administrative entity changes, this distinction proved crucial to developing and implementing an innovative welfare-to-work program.

El Paso Community College Involvement in Welfare Programs

In Texas, there are over fifty community and technical colleges, and most minority and low-income Texans start their higher education in a community college. El Paso Community College (EPCC), located in the large border city of El Paso in far west Texas, serves around eighteen thousand credit students annually. Eighty percent of these students are Hispanic, and 62 percent receive Pell grants to cover the cost of their education. The community of El Paso, home to over 700,000 residents, is the fifth poorest city in the United States.

EPCC has designed and delivered special programs for welfare recipients since the 1980s, mostly due to the strong interest of several department heads rather than the institution as a whole. In the 1980s, EPCC developed a life skills program for welfare recipients, Project Forward, that a number of programs across Texas used. EPCC provided the statewide training for Project Forward's implementation and worked closely with the programs around the state that were implementing the curriculum with their welfare clients.

EPCC also offered education and job training programs for welfare recipients, culminating in Project Pride, which provided a stratified, multi-service approach to serving welfare recipients at all educational levels, from those requiring literacy and ESL courses to associate degree candidates. EPCC created a small training center offering twenty to twenty-five hours a week of intensive workplace ESL for dislocated workers who were primarily non-English-speaking women with elementary-level education in Mexico. Once the center was created, other non-English-speaking special populations were also served. At the same time, welfare recipients enrolled in college credit programs achieved their twenty hours of mandatory training by signing in and out of big red binders placed in each college library. College staff picked up these attendance sheets and delivered them to the local welfare agency biweekly—a low-tech, low-cost solution to a twenty-hour participation mandate.

Developing a New Program in the Context of Welfare Reform

The state's new SSF presented attractive opportunities to a small group of individuals at EPCC who were concerned about the effect of work-first welfare reform on poor women and their children in El Paso. The state administered the SSF program through the Texas Workforce Commission (TWC), a new agency created out of the old Texas Department of Commerce, Texas Employment Commission, and Texas Department of Human Services. It was responsible for employment services, programs for dislocated workers like Trade Adjustment Assistance, unemployment compensation, and other federal job training dollars for welfare to work. TWC, however, had placed the administration of the SSF in a separate department along with another state-funded program, the Skills Development Fund. This insulated the program from the rapid and often chaotic changes overtaking the federal welfare-to-work programs.

When EPCC went looking for an employer to be a partner in creating a state-funded self-sufficiency project, it was not by happenstance that the YWCA was the first and only partner it approached. The EPCC-YWCA partnership was already well established. The YWCA is the largest employer of child care workers in the area, and EPCC is the largest supplier of trained child care workers. In fact, child development is the largest occupational program at EPCC and produces the greatest number of associate degrees each year. The child development program offers a shorter child development associate (CDA) credential training program, which takes six months to one year to complete. The CDA program is fully articulated to the associate degree program, and the associate degree program is fully articulated to the New Mexico State University (NMSU) bachelor degree program in home and consumer science. With the NMSU bachelor degree, a graduate can teach school or work in occupations like social work. By law in Texas, college classes must be taught in English, but the EPCC faculty is virtually all bilingual, and classes are often taught in English with considerable supplemental Spanish. The child care industry in El Paso employs mostly bilingual and monolingual Spanish speakers.

The YWCA in El Paso is one of the largest in the United States and plays a large role in serving women and families in the community. As the local Child Care Management Service (CCMS), the El Paso YWCA places thousands of low-income children into day care each year. The YWCA itself offers many quality child care programs in every area of the city, as well as vetting other child care providers for inclusion on the CCMS master list. The YWCA hires dozens of child care workers every year and provides its own ongoing training, required for all child care industry workers to maintain a state provider license. In Texas, the regulations for operating a child care center are surprisingly strict, and the YWCA takes its responsibility seriously. The YWCA had been conducting internal discussions about creating a training center to supply the YWCA with entry-level child care workers. The YWCA and EPCC decided to work together to create this training center.

Many welfare recipients are attracted to the child care industry. As mothers, caring for children is something about which they have intimate knowledge and experience. Child care also offers opportunities for self-employment in one's own home as a registered home provider. Most welfare recipients in El Paso place great value on staying home and caring for their own children. The population of El Paso is 78 percent Hispanic, mostly of Mexican origin, and the labor force participation rate for women is lower than in other areas of the country. Although welfare payments in Texas are only $201 per month for a family of three, ranking forty-seventh in the nation, Texas welfare mothers prize the availability of health care through Medicaid for their children.

The major disadvantage to child care is its low pay, barely above minimum wage. Realistically, a family of three still will live below the poverty line on a minimum wage job, and losing Medicaid is a stiff penalty to pay for employment. Under PRWORA, newly employed welfare recipients can continue receiving Medicaid for time periods that allow them to become established in the job market. In Texas, Medicaid is available for up to eighteen months after employment.

It is no coincidence that the small group of women who developed and implemented the YWCA Child Care Training Center were mostly single parents. All believed that a training center for child care workers should offer not just an entry-level job to welfare recipients but the opportunity to earn college credentials that could immediately be applied to a college associate degree or the CDA credential. The focus of the program was on entry-level employment as a child care worker, but in a job that supported one's goals of continuing in college.

Welfare recipients live in a culture of poverty, where it is difficult to plan for more than one month at a time. The idea of earning a bachelor degree and becoming a teacher, social worker, or businesswomen would be irrelevant to a woman who was more focused on how to buy food for her children that night. Welfare recipients do not see themselves as the creative, competent people that they are. No one lives on the $201 a month that Texas provides in welfare. Welfare recipients are a very entrepreneurial lot, and each woman has a myriad ways of supplementing her income. Common ways in El Paso include making and selling food such as burritos; crafting ceramics and piñatas; making candy; buying cheap household goods in Mexico and selling them in El Paso door to door; selling Avon products; babysitting; dancing in nightclubs; engaging in occasional prostitution; earning commissions in barely disguised pyramid schemes; and working as maids. They also get money from family members, friends, and male partners. In fact, the new participation and attendance requirements under PRWORA actually interfere with a welfare mother's ability to support her family. If one assumes that a welfare mother is spending her time watching soap operas and sleeping all day, thirty-five hours a week of planned job search or training may seem reasonable and warranted, as do strict attendance requirements. But in fact, welfare mothers are very busy people raising the money their children need to live. Program designers must become aware of this situation.

The fully articulated child development program, the first in the country, offered the opportunity to reach employment and education goals in small, attainable pieces with multiple exit points that provided credentials for the employment market at better than minimum wage. The puzzle was how to do this in a way that would allow welfare recipients to meet the requirements of welfare reform and its work-first philosophy and still begin the educational pathway that was their only route out of poverty.

This is where the state of Texas SSF became far more attractive than the federal programs. Because the SSF was created without regard to what was happening in the federal workforce development system, restrictions and regulations were few. An SSF project initially did not have to follow the limitations and requirements of the PICs or the Department of Human Services where welfare was administered. The advantages were enormous. If an interested woman was a current welfare recipient, she qualified for SSF programs. She did not have to be in the right service category, she did not have to be JTPA or Workforce Investment Act (WIA) certified and accepted for training, and she was not on a waiting list with two hundred names ahead of her. All she needed was a current TANF letter. With the early implementation of WIA and PRWORA, a major reorganization of the welfare and workforce development systems in Texas under House Bill 863, and the state's decision to fund a statewide contractor to start work-first programs throughout Texas, local chaos reigned within the existing systems. The YWCA submitted a self-sufficiency proposal, with EPCC as the training provider and the YWCA as the employer.

Program Design

The program design incorporated the college philosophy that each educational milestone is simply one more step on the pathway of higher education. The first step was the twelve-week training program itself, which was housed in an day care center. Students attended three hours of classroom instruction daily and worked as interns in the day care center for another three hours. Each was assigned to an experienced YWCA child care teacher, who was given a salary bonus to serve as a mentor and on-the-job trainer for the student. In Texas, child care workers are required by law to possess a GED or high school diploma. About a third of the students lacked a GED and attended additional hours in the day care center classroom to work on their English or Spanish GED with a college instructor. Most others had a GED; very few had a high school diploma.

The child care worker course consisted of 180 classroom contact hours with 180 hours of concurrent internship in the child care center each twelve-week session. The curriculum for the course integrated English basic skills into the child development content, and each assignment included reading, writing, oral discussion, and listening skills. The curriculum included the content of the first two credit courses in child development at EPCC. This allowed students to earn credit hours that were articulated into EPCC's CDA and associate degree child development program.

Ninety percent of the students were limited English proficient and spoke Spanish as their first language. Some students did their written assignments in Spanish. No homework was assigned, recognizing that each woman left class to spend the rest of the day caring for her children and earning extra income. When welfare students entered the program, the articulated credit was meaningless to them. The EPCC instructor and the YWCA training center coordinator, along with invited guest speakers, explicitly pushed the message that the students were now in college and were capable of earning a CDA credential. In the first weeks of each session, the students were bused to an EPCC campus for a college student identification card. The purpose was to accustom them to defining themselves as college students, not welfare clients.

During the program, they were encouraged to think of themselves as completing the first step in earning their CDA credential, which (it was emphasized) covered most of the requirements of an associate degree. They were encouraged to think of themselves as future day care teachers (CDA level), day care center directors or owners, school teachers, or social workers. These occupations were emphasized because welfare recipients tend to be aware of a limited number of occupations (those they come into constant contact with) and because the fully articulated career path they had entered would qualify them for these specific occupations. Most important, altruistic occupations like teaching and social work allowed them to see themselves as helpful people who could use their experiences to help others out of their difficult life situations.

Students also listened to guest speakers who talked openly about how abusive relationships and abusers keep a woman down and make her feel badly about herself. Talks like this came from women who had been in those situations and had fought their way out of them. Both male and female speakers talked about self-esteem, dressing for the job, work ethics, and numerous other topics. Toward the end of the program, the students were taken back to an EPCC campus for a special new-student orientation. They filled out and submitted college application and financial aid forms, met their assigned counselor and some of the child development teachers, and learned about EPCC services. They were scheduled for placement testing and made follow-up appointments with the counselor for class advising. At this point, the articulated credit hours took on great meaning for the students, an importance that the college credit hours lacked just twelve weeks earlier.

The first cohort of students resulted in only three who enrolled at EPCC the next semester. With subsequent groups, approximately half enrolled at the college. Several have now earned their CDA credential and are working on their associate degree. The program is tracking the participants' progress through the college, a feature that was not included in the original program model.

SSF training and funding end when the student graduates and enters employment. Welfare benefits end too, and assistance for child care and Medicaid end in twelve to eighteen months. With work first, the federal and state workforce development programs do not support additional education and training. Many program graduates have been stymied because they do not qualify for Pell grants.

To date, the program, now in its third year and enrolling four groups of fifteen students each year, has ninety-three graduates out of one hundred enrolled participants. Seventy-eight entered employment, one is a full-time university student, eight passed the child care worker training course but have not yet passed the GED and hence cannot work in a day care center (some are working elsewhere), and ten were never hired. Seventy-four remain employed.

Navigating Legislative Mandates and the Agencies

The YWCA and EPCC had long histories of working with the various workforce development agencies. EPCC, in fact, had been the largest provider of training services to JTPA. Employees in the different institutions had worked together for years and often were friends. A constant employment pathway between the YWCA, EPCC, and the different workforce development and welfare agencies was well established. For example, many caseworkers and child care mentors had been EPCC students, and several of the YWCA staff involved were current instructors at EPCC. As a result of these relationships, there was a shared commitment to making the program work, no matter what institutional obstacles might come in the way, as well as a confidence in the quality of each other's services.

Recruitment for the program was to be provided by the private industry council and the Texas Department of Human Services (DHS). In practice, this meant that virtually all student referrals came from DHS and Choices, the Texas welfare-to-work program. The JTPA eligibility determination, assessment, and referral system worked very slowly and inefficiently, whereas DHS sent recruitment flyers to thousands of eligible welfare recipients with a few weeks' notice. After several unproductive starts, the most effective recruitment method turned out to be the blanket of flyers along with presentations to groups of caseworkers in both the Choices program and DHS, followed by a week-long open house for interested welfare recipients at the YWCA child care center, where the training would take place.

Because EPCC had provided other special programs for welfare recipients in the past, whereas this was the first such program for the YWCA, EPCC was able to anticipate many of the issues that arose. The state was simultaneously implementing the work-first program through a for-profit contractor. PIC counselors and Choices case managers were told that all TANF recipients must go through work-first programs before they could be considered for training. However, the contractor had hundreds of TANF recipients to work through, and most were just names on a lengthy waiting list. The independence that the SSF provided meant that EPCC and the YWCA were not constrained by this requirement, and neither was DHS. Recruitment was accomplished without regard for this requirement and with the anticipation that by the time the contractor called the students up, they would have finished the child care worker training program and be employed. This is exactly what happened. When an occasional active student was called for the work-first program, the Choices caseworkers found ways to allow the student to stay in the training program without sanctions.

Through experience, caseworkers learned to send new students to the PIC after they were enrolled in the training program. Although the PIC, EPCC, and the YWCA had signed a memorandum of understanding that gave the PIC a role in recruiting and providing supportive services, in practice few recipients sent to the PIC ever made it through the process of certification and returned for the program. Sending students to the PIC after they were safely in the training program helped ensure that they would not get lost along the way.

What Works

Experiences led to several practical rules for the instructor and staff:

- Do not lend money to students.
- Follow up on every missed class immediately.
- Do not alter the attendance sheets sent to each welfare caseworker.

- Do not gossip about students or reveal their confidences to anyone unless legally obligated to (child abuse).
- Do not allow students to bully other students.
- Do not say bad things about PIC or DHS or Choices staff to students.
- Do not permit threatening behaviors in the classroom or work site.

To keep students involved and successful, we also learned the following:

- Be caring and friendly.
- Be encouraging, and repeat messages of social cohesion be endlessly patient.
- Be a good role model.
- Offer praise when earned.
- Set strict standards for attendance and tardiness, and then excuse incidents privately to individual students.
- Refer to better-equipped services or agencies when appropriate, and follow up with the student.
- Keep class fun, but emphasize hard work through a strong curriculum.
- Repeat future-oriented messages.

Overall, this program works for many reasons. Everyone involved in the program believes that the operative goal is a living wage and economic self-sufficiency for a single parent and her children, not just employment. Our goal is to move a family out of poverty, and the staff and instructors from both the YWCA and EPCC possess the strong belief based on personal experience that only higher education can enable a female-headed household to escape poverty. These core beliefs led EPCC and the YWCA to design around and sometimes in spite of goals laid out in the state and federal legislation. This effort was immensely aided by the professionals in the welfare and workforce development systems, who had to meet their legislatively mandated goals as well as ours, and the program participants themselves, who presented us with many challenges every day and yet persevered, despite all their barriers.

Kathleen Bombach is former director of the Literacy and Workforce Development Center at El Paso Community College in El Paso, Texas. She now works with nonprofit and public agencies in El Paso to develop and provide education and workforce development programs.

9

This chapter presents the story of a successful welfare reform program and explains how one upstate New York county and community college created a unique and comprehensive methodology.

The JOBSplus! Program: Successful Work First Through a Family-Based Approach

Patricia C. Higgins, Janice Mayne, Patricia Deacon, Elena LaComb

Onondaga Community College (OCC) in upstate New York, near Syracuse, has been administering the county's employment program for welfare recipients for the past seven years. Prior to 1994, Onondaga County focused on a sequential model of education, training, and job search for individuals in the JOBSplus! program. OCC had been participating by providing case management to college students on public assistance and vocational training in the form of certificate and degree programs. Gradually, the college began doing more of the case management functions previously done by the Department of Social Services (DSS). These functions included authorizing child care and transportation, entering data on New York State's Welfare Management System, and participating in the conciliation and sanction processes.

Approximately three years prior to the passing of the PRWORA legislation, the college, the county, and several other agencies came together to discuss revamping the entire welfare employment program. Before specific programs were discussed, a set of principles concerning workforce preparation strategies was developed to guide local efforts in preparing welfare recipients for the existing labor market:

Workforce preparation activities should be authentic and replicate to the greatest extent possible actual labor force conditions.
By combining work experience with classroom education or training, the pace at which individuals will acquire the needed work-related skills will be accelerated.

Within specified parameters for participation, individuals should be given the greatest possible degree of self-direction in selecting opportunities that will move them the most rapidly to economic independence.

These principles are still in effect today.

With the agencies having agreed on the guiding principles, what remained to be done was to develop a program to implement them. This was no small task, but in March 1995, the doors of the JOBSplus! Learn-to-Work Center opened. This center provides comprehensive training and family-oriented support services for welfare recipients, including life skills and work skills.

Since that time, the public assistance caseload in Onondaga County has been reduced by almost 60 percent. There have been 16,368 jobs recorded that were filled by individuals involved with our program. A sample of individuals who found employment five years ago shows the following promising results: 92 percent have their cases currently closed, 3 percent have cases currently open with earned income, and 5 percent have cases open with no earned income.

In light of these encouraging outcomes, we at the JOBSplus! program remain committed to a work-first approach. To further improve outcomes, this approach needs to be holistic and provide opportunities for individuals and families to move off welfare into jobs that will bring self-sufficiency. What follows are the best practices developed by the program for an effective, family-based work-first approach.

Family-Centered Projects

As people begin to think about employment, issues arise that must be addressed. To that end, we have developed several projects, each dealing with a specific issue that affects the ability of individuals to look for, secure, and retain jobs.

Specialized Case Management. Long-term welfare recipients frequently face a multitude of serious issues. The most common are mental illness and substance abuse. In an effort to learn more about the services available and to create a plan of action for integrating employment services into the therapeutic arena, we arranged a series of meetings with local providers of mental health, substance abuse, and child protection services. Through the course of these meetings, we found that the providers were not necessarily in agreement on the role of vocational rehabilitation in recovery planning. We learned that through the combined effects of regulatory and funding restrictions and different therapeutic approaches, the systems tended to operate independent of one another. Finally, we learned that the systems rarely provided a follow-along service; if the client voluntarily left counseling or a rehabilitation program, the provider was powerless to persuade the client to return. The providers were interested in the possibility of integrating our vocational services and our ability to require participation into their therapeutic plans.

From these meetings arose a realization that intensive case management, whereby a case manager assesses the family as a unit, provides clients with the means to access therapeutic services, and coordinates the services of all the involved agencies, was a critical component in helping job seekers with multiple issues begin to address those issues within a holistic and manageable framework. In other words, through case management, all providers would have full information and could work together to provide needed services in an integrated fashion to facilitate progress toward the goals of recovery and self-sufficiency.

Three intensive case management programs were initiated, targeting families who are mandated to receive child abuse prevention services, who are in alcohol or drug rehabilitation, or who are mentally ill or developmentally disabled. These programs provide continuity and coordination of service to families across a multitude of services and institutions, including schools and the courts. In spite of the fact that some of these families present truly heartbreaking situations, through case management there are now parents who are employed and children who are being returned to the home. As evidenced by this service, welfare reform has facilitated cooperation and understanding among systems, to the benefit of the clients.

Housing Project. Public assistance recipients may live in a variety of unstable housing situations, particularly in an urban setting. Apartments may be substandard, the neighborhood may be unsafe, and for those leaving alcohol or drug rehabilitation facilities, returning to the old neighborhood can precipitate relapse. It was our assumption that unstable housing prevented job seekers from concentrating on job search and job retention.

Onondaga County also has some isolated rural communities. Job seekers living in those areas frequently do not have access to public transportation or job opportunities.

We contracted with a nonprofit agency to provide services to job seekers who indicate a need to find more suitable housing. The service includes temporary housing for those being evicted, moving services, furniture, assistance with finding appropriate housing, access to subsidies, and tenant education.

Living Well Workshops. These workshops target people who move very frequently. Screening criteria scan for various causes of moves, such as unpaid rent or excessive noise. When identified, individuals are referred to a Living Well Workshop. Attendance is required at four ninety-minute sessions.

The primary goal of the Living Well Workshop is to help every person become a better-informed tenant. Topics include learning how to get along with landlords, maintaining a healthy living environment, finding information, living safely, and being a good tenant and neighbor. The hope is that by addressing these types of issues, graduates from the classes will stabilize their residential lives, and this stabilization may result in successful and steady employment.

Domestic Violence Project. While the Department of Social Services screens all applicants for domestic violence issues and exempts those who are in a crisis situation from employment requirements, there are still job seekers who have not identified themselves as victims of domestic violence but are in fact dealing with an abusive situation.

A local domestic violence assistance program provides on-site counseling at the JOBSplus! office. It is our belief that although clients may be fearful of accessing services directly because of fear of discovery, they will be able to access counseling and referral at our office without raising the abuser's suspicion. A counselor is stationed at the office two days each week and is on call at all times should a client in crisis request assistance.

Legal Assistance Project. We frequently hear from job seekers that they are fearful of taking jobs and leaving public assistance because of outstanding debts and other legal problems. Public assistance often provides a shield against creditors and certain life situations. Once a client leaves public assistance, the shield is gone, and the client may be besieged by creditors, spouses seeking child custody, and others. This is a catch-22 situation because the client cannot afford qualified legal assistance in resolving these issues.

We contracted with a local nonprofit legal services agency to address this problem. We refer clients for assistance with a variety of legal issues, ranging from bankruptcy, child custody, divorce, and disputed bills, to traffic infractions, criminal matters, and juvenile delinquency issues. In order to keep the service completely confidential, this contract is based on a flat fee structure, and outcomes are tracked only in the aggregate.

Clothing for Kids Project. Staff identified an ongoing need to have children's clothes available. As they meet with job seekers, they are confronted with children not adequately outfitted for weather conditions. Other life situations (such as eviction, domestic violence, and fires) can result in insufficient clothing. This situation launched the Kids Clothing Closet. Staff generously donated gently used and new items for infants and children, and a local church adopted JOBSplus! for its Christmas project, putting together an array of new and hand-made winter clothes.

Along with the children's clothing closet, the agency's staff created a school supplies box. Staff members donated pencils, crayons, pads, rules, scissors, and many other supplies, so job seekers' children could start the school year with adequate materials. Supplies continue to be available throughout the school year as students run out.

Job Readiness Projects

Helping people look for work is not as simple as telling them to get a job, even in a booming economy and even if the projects already noted are in place. It is also not as simple as putting them in training programs and expecting that they will successfully complete the training, find employment, and stay on the job. There are many aspects to job readiness. JOBSplus! provides programs and services to prepare job seekers for employment.

Preemployment Workshops. Many public assistance recipients are exempt from employment requirements due to permanent or temporary disabilities or limitations. One way to connect with these people has been through the Preemployment Workshop. Approximately ten to twelve people gather for ten two-hour sessions over a five-week period.

In a softly structured format, participants are invited to discuss their questions and share their thoughts, opinions, and observations. Although the workshop curriculum does not focus directly on employment-related topics, discussions are always contextualized within an employment framework. Instructors help participants consider alternative vocational choices as a means to heighten their awareness of welfare time limits. The sessions create the opportunity for participants to practice goal setting, participate in group discussions, and learn more about themselves. Positive outcomes include, achievement of perfect attendance, lessening of the sense of isolation, production of a resumé for some, and referral to vocational counseling agencies.

Job Clubs. Job Clubs are always designed with one goal in mind: successful entry into employment. Sessions begin every Monday and may continue for up to three weeks. Daily classes run for approximately five hours and include structured job search throughout the entire component.

Every participant composes a resumé, which is transformed into a professional-looking document by agency staff. Emphasis is placed on learning effective job search techniques and also on acquiring the essential skills to retain a job.

Resumé Preparation. Resumé preparation services are available to all program participants. Those not participating in the Job Club who need this service can meet with a job coach instructor to help them work through the drafting process.

Staff members type all resumés, save them, and print copies as needed. Storage ensures that people can update information and make changes on their documents. The importance of having a resumé is emphasized to all JOBSplus! participants. Presenting a professional document to a potential employer can make the difference between a decision to hire or not.

Work Experience and Job Seeker Recognition. The work experience component of the program is critical for anyone not yet employed. Three hundred sites around the community provide assignments that are handpicked to suit individual needs, talents, skill levels, languages, and employment goals. Sites offer a full variety of work environments and are a reflection of the types of entry-level employment available throughout the community, including health care, educational, clerical, landscaping, food service, retail, and maintenance.

Most participants are assigned for three to six months for twenty to twenty-five hours weekly. This activity is scheduled in conjunction with others, including job readiness, training, and employment. Staff are on call to help with issues that arise on site. Staff also regularly visit sites to check in with participants and site supervisors. This allows them to resolve any issues, provide job leads, and monitor client progress. Although work experience is not intended to be a lead-in to employment at the sites, in some cases it has happened. In every case, it is a springboard to employment; participants are building skills, networking, adding to their resumés, and overcoming their own individual barriers to employment.

To celebrate success along the way, we hold quarterly job seeker recognition ceremonies. This program was initiated by staff who saw the need to encourage those who do well in work experience and who are making significant progress toward their goals. These events are totally paid for by staff. Staff also hold bake sales and other fundraisers, and they nominate the individuals who will receive certificates of achievement and other small gifts. Also invited are site supervisors, who are recognized for their roles as mentors.

Child Care. By far the largest need addressed is the coverage of child care expenses. JOBSplus! covers these costs whenever a participant is attending an activity or working. We provide assistance through the local Child Care Council in locating appropriate providers. In addition, providers not registered with New York State and considered to be of an informal status (family or friends) are rigorously examined in order to be approved to provide these services. Once employment is found, we work in tandem with other parts of Social Services to ensure no interruption of coverage until the next source of transitional benefits is established. We strive to help parents make good decisions about child care and backup child care, so they will be free to focus on work and reach the larger goals they have set for themselves and their families.

Transportation. The next largest need is transportation. We offer a comprehensive bus pass program for participants in activities throughout the county. Most individuals receive an unlimited pass, which allows them to use the city bus system not only to participate in mandated activities but also to conduct other necessary business. Where participants have vehicles and no other reliable mode of transportation exists, we offer reimbursement for expenses and sometimes cover repairs. We cover the cost of transportation until the first paychecks are received.

JOBSplus! Clothing Closet. The JOBSplus! Clothing Closet was created to meet the need of job seekers who did not have appropriate attire for interviews, work experience assignments, or employment. A rudimentary plan was developed and implemented by staff, who donated from their own wardrobes. Next, local thrift and consignment shops donated merchandise they were willing to write off at the end of the selling season. In related activities, we have contracted with image consultants to work with participants to address their individual issues. We have also involved staff in a fashion show, where they modeled apparel from the Clothing Closet in order to promote its use and the importance of appropriate business attire.

Workplace Education. An important foundation of the work-first philosophy is that learning must be contextualized in a work setting. As a next step to basic job readiness programming, we piloted a contextualized learning experience. The job seeker is assigned to twenty hours of work experience each week, in addition to fifteen hours of classroom literacy instruction. Each week, the instructor visits each class participant at his or her worksite and observes the tasks the job seeker is performing. Back in the classroom, the instructor provides ongoing literacy instruction revolving around the work experience tasks. A classic example is the job seeker who was in a food service work experience assignment. The instructor was able to use the large quantities of sandwiches the job seeker was preparing to demonstrate multiplication and division concepts. This program has been highly successful in placing participants in paid employment at higher levels than the job seekers might otherwise have achieved given their initial literacy levels.

Job Retention and Self-Sufficiency

Economic independence involves getting the job, keeping the job, and moving up. Most of us are not still working at our first jobs. We worked and maybe worked our way up to a better position. Perhaps we looked around and found that with additional training, we would be eligible for promotions or for different jobs completely. We need to make sure that our participants also have opportunities for upward mobility. We need to make sure not only that the first job lasts, but also that it is not the last, or the only, job.

Infoline. The JOBSplus! Infoline was designed with employed participants in mind. Unfortunately, individuals who need information about transitional benefits or services sometimes get passed around from department to department. This specialized telephone line is promoted among employed participants as a one-stop resource with a team of staff experts on call to answer a full range of questions. They have information from various departments and other resources in the community. If information is not available, the staff member is charged with finding it and getting back to the caller instead of redirecting the call. This service has encouraged people not to give up in frustration but to be able instead to access the benefits and information they need to remain employed.

Local Earned Income Credit. The local earned-income credit (LEIC) provides a reward to those who are working. Anyone who has worked full time for ninety days and whose public assistance case closes during that time can receive an LEIC of $150. There is an added benefit to the LEIC as well. At the time we verify eligibility for the reward, we also review all available transitional benefits with the client and assist him or her with applying for them. It is very common that once people leave public assistance, they do not access the benefits to which they are entitled. The LEIC helps ensure they do receive everything they should to supplement their incomes. There is a second LEIC, which is an additional $150 payable to anyone who continues to work an additional ninety days. Clients who have received the LEIC report they use the money for school clothes, holiday presents, and other purchases that might normally strain the family budget.

Employee Transportation Projects. Several federal and state grants have been combined to provide a complete array of transportation services to employed recipients and former recipients of public assistance. Clients may attend comprehensive driver training classes, which enables them to get their driver's permit, get on-the-road experience, and take the licensing test. This is probably one of the most popular programs offered. Once licensed, employed participants may apply for subsidized, no-interest car loans. For instance, clients may purchase a car valued at up to $4,600 and pay as little as $120 a month for eighteen months. Added benefits include car maintenance classes, car care kits, memberships in the American Automobile Association, and child car seats. Repairs are free, as is liability insurance, as long as payments are made regularly.

We have contracted with the local public transportation company, CENTRO, to provide mobility management services. Any employed job seeker can go to the Mobility Management Center and receive a transportation plan. The center provides information about bus routes and in the absence of public transportation provides van or taxi service—or whatever else it takes to get the new employee to work. Eventually, the job seeker may wish to consider the car loan program. Guaranteed rides home, in the event of an emergency, are also provided through the program.

Employer-Specific Projects. Certain employers in the community hire large numbers of public assistance recipients and provide an opportunity for on-the-job interventions to promote retention. A good example is a local nursing home facility. We arranged to have staff who were well versed in postemployment issues and transitional benefits outstationed on a regular basis at the nursing home. Employees were encouraged to visit and learn about benefits they could receive, as well as to discuss any problems they were having on the job. A large number of employees took advantage of this service, and many were assisted with a variety of issues.

Computer Classes and Extended Hours. In order to provide maximum access to the services and programs, JOBSplus! began providing evening hours. The agency is open until 7:30 P.M. every Wednesday. In order to make it possible for parents to take care of appointments or attend workshops during the evening hours, two children's activities specialists are available. In addition, children can have dinner at the agency. One of the primary goals for the evening program is to provide supplemental skills acquisition. A series of evening computer classes has been developed. Topics vary over a four-week cycle and include introductions to Word and Windows, as well as resumé preparation.

Another evening activity is the Your Next Step seminar. This workshop series is designed for public assistance recipients who are employed but still receive a small cash grant. Topics include strategies to increase income, benefits available after case closure, and computer instruction.

Onondaga Community College Classes. JOBSplus! has worked closely with its parent, Onondaga Community College, to develop its downtown location as an extension site. To that end, the college offers an array of classes during weekday evening hours. The attraction to downtown workers and urban residents is building gradually. Ten classes are offered each semester.

There are numerous advantages to this model: convenience, increased enrollments, opportunity for TANF graduates to attend college, and community involvement by the college (the main campus is located in a suburban area).

Upgrade-Training Subsidies. We used the flexibility of the welfare-to-work grants to make upgrade training more accessible to those who are employed. The upgrade training subsidies can operate in one of two ways. An employee who has an opportunity for promotion within a company or for a better job with another company can be subsidized in the new position at a rate up to 100 percent of gross wages for up to six months. A job developer works with the employer to arrange the subsidy. This program provides incentive to employers to consider promoting eligible applicants.

An employee who wishes to take training or education classes but is finding it difficult to juggle full-time employment with family responsibilities can take time off from work to take classes. The missed time from work is reimbursed to either the employee or the employer, so that the employee sees no difference in take-home pay and the employer loses only the time the employee is not at work.

Gifford Scholarships. In 1999, the Rosamond Gifford Foundation, a major charitable donor in the Syracuse area, gave the largest endowment in its history to Onondaga Community College. This innovative fund was created in response to the need to help employed individuals who were currently in receipt of TANF or who had recently closed their cases to obtain upgrade training and education. The funding allows scholarship funds, for any accredited program, to be awarded for tuition, child care, transportation, and books to support students in their vocational pursuits. Recently, eligibility requirements have been expanded to include low-income families from one- or two-parent households whose income level also renders them eligible for other benefits, including the Home Energy Assistance Program, Food Stamps, transitional child care, or Medicaid.

Scholarship holders must certify that they will continue working and not increase their financial need in order to qualify for temporary assistance. However, as an incentive to increase employer support of this program, funds are available for employers in the event they should have to pay a temporary worker for the hours the scholarship holder must participate in training.

Coupon Books. In seeking a concise and catchy way to impart to TANF participants the full scope of services and benefits available to them as they seek and find employment, we created the Temporary Assistance Coupon Book for distribution. Each booklet contains cut-out coupons featuring many of the programs described that are available at no cost.

Breaking the Cycle

Because we can now also work with individuals who may not be on assistance but whose income is below 200 percent of the poverty level, we are reaching more deeply into the community. Through a family-centered approach, we are able to implement some prevention projects that we hope will help the next generation.

High School Employment Readiness Workshops. JOBSplus! staff have incorporated many activities that are designed to prevent development of a relationship with public assistance or to abbreviate an individual's linkage to the system. One strategy is the provision of job search preparation classes to high school students. Teenagers do not receive job search instruction from high school faculty on a regular basis. JOBSplus! staff reach into city high schools to provide students instruction about job search, interviewing, writing applications, and appropriate dress. In addition, resumés or personal data sheets may be produced.

Some employers have worked with the high schools to coordinate on-site interviews when the sessions conclude. In all cases, teenagers are better prepared for a successful job search. The long-term effects may result in more stable labor force attachment and fewer case openings.

Career Path to Success. In 1999, the City of Syracuse and Onondaga County governments sought solutions to increasing gun violence by local teenagers. Both governmental entities became more closely and actively involved with the federally funded Partnership to Reduce Juvenile Gun Violence. JOBSplus! began to provide individualized job search skills development assistance.

The agency moved quickly to the development of a model that pulls together the community college, the Workforce Investment Agency, and local government. Career Path to Success is designed to provide fifteen to twenty high-risk youths with exposure to a college environment. A ten-week early evening session resulted in acquisition of eight college credits for students completing the project. The experience provided them with a unique opportunity to expand their horizons. They left the streets for a while, associated with a wide variety of students (sometimes from other neighborhoods or gang affiliations), and had a chance to study in a structured academic environment.

Teen ACE Awards. The Teen ACE Awards Program was created to reward fourth- through twelfth-grade students who were attending and doing well in school and for making contributions to the community. Students must ultimately demonstrate performance in the areas of achievement, character, and excellence, from which the acronym ACE was created.

The Teen ACE Awards are used to fund eligible youth in a variety of initiatives, including one week's free attendance at the summer program of their choice. This includes any recreational, sports, or educational program within New York State. Other contests have included family passes to sports, recreational, or cultural events in the community. We have also awarded personal computers and printers, books, and music and sports equipment.

Conclusion

At JOBSplus! the role of the community college in welfare reform is comprehensive, holistic, flexible, and family-centered. We are part of the community and are concerned with case closings and public funds. We also see ourselves as responsible for ensuring that those who leave the system are afforded opportunities for advancement so that poverty will not continue to be a way of life. Because of its history of community involvement, its role as a provider of education and training, its ability to change, and its connections with local businesses, Onondaga Community College is in a unique position to lead local welfare reform efforts. Because of the success locally, the college is also in a unique position to influence other communities by serving as a model for family-centered welfare to work.

PATRICIA C. HIGGINS is director of JOBSplus! in Syracuse, New York.

JANICE MAYNE is associate director of JOBSplus! in Syracuse, New York.

PATRICIA DEACON is Learn-to-Work service coordinator of JOBSplus! in Syracuse, New York.

ELENA LaCOMB is a team leader of JOBSplus! in Syracuse, New York.

10

This chapter presents additional information on welfare to work at community colleges, including information on students, state and local initiatives, and national trends.

Sources and Information: The Community College and Welfare Reform

Katalin Szelènyi

The year 2001 marks the fifth anniversary of the Personal Responsibility and Work Opportunity Reconciliation Act (PRWORA). This federal legislation, emphasizing involvement in job-related activities and restricting the amount of time a welfare recipient can engage in vocational education to a maximum of twelve months, has significantly altered the community college role in providing welfare-related education and training. At community colleges, shorter-term training programs with heightened focus on employment have increasingly become the common mode of providing instruction for welfare recipients. Furthermore, the new law, by giving states a high degree of flexibility in defining work activities, including vocational education, within their programs, has also created considerable variation among states, resulting in diverse patterns of training options across the country (Grubb, Badway, Bell, and Castellano, 1999).

This chapter outlines documents in the ERIC database describing state and community college–level responses to welfare reform.[1] The publications reviewed address questions related to the welfare student population, state policy initiatives, and emerging educational programs at community colleges, including short-term programs, adult basic and literacy education, and programs undertaken at specific community colleges.

The Welfare Student Population

Community colleges have long been involved in providing education and training to welfare recipients, a student population with a number of academic

New Directions for Community Colleges, no. 116, Winter 2001 © John Wiley, & Sons, Inc.

and personal barriers that impede educational success. Welfare reform has had various impacts on the enrollment of welfare recipients nationwide and on services aimed at these students.

Literacy and Basic Skills. Some of the obstacles to employment that welfare recipients most frequently experience are "lack of transportation, lack of social networks, low educational attainment, racial discrimination, health problems for themselves or their children, the demands of parenting young children, lack of work experience, and unavailability of affordable child care" (Strawn, 1998, para. 16). However, considering personal and family barriers only, low basic skills represent the most important impediment to finding and maintaining employment by a welfare recipient.

Community colleges have traditionally engaged in providing basic and literacy education to their students who are receiving welfare benefits. Because welfare reform has considerably scaled back the capacity of colleges to provide basic and literacy education, given the emphasis on job skills, it is important to consider the educational skills and literacy levels of the welfare student body. A large proportion of welfare recipients possess very low educational and skill levels (Hayes, 1999). Findings from the 1992 National Adult Literacy Survey (NALS) indicate that measured on a five-point scale, over a third to almost half of all welfare recipients demonstrated literacy skills at the lowest level, and around one-third of the welfare population performed at the second lowest level. On average, welfare recipients performed at lower levels than unskilled laborers and assemblers. Furthermore, demonstrating that neither gender or ethnic background was a significant determiner of literacy performance for welfare recipients, the study's findings indicated that the differences existing between males and females, whites and blacks, and whites and Hispanics are smaller than in the population at large (Barton and Jenkins, 1995).

A national welfare-to-work survey of nearly 400 community colleges conducted by the American Association of Community Colleges (AACC) in 1998 indicated that low levels of literacy skills are among the most pertinent issues characterizing welfare students at community colleges. Sixty-four percent of responding institutions highlighted literacy and numerical skills as the most important area for improvement in their welfare-to-work student population (Kienzl, 1999). Two other skill areas in which community colleges found their welfare students lacking were personal management skills (63 percent) and interpersonal skills (52.9 percent).

Enrollment. Research findings are somewhat inconclusive as to the impact of welfare reform on the number of welfare recipients attending education and training programs at community colleges. Many community colleges reported significant decreases in their student population of welfare recipients. In the Massachusetts community college system, welfare enrollments fell from 8,000 to 4,000 within two years (Schmidt, 1998). A similar decrease occurred in the Washington Community and Technical College System. Between 1996 and 1997, the number of students receiving public assistance dropped by 23 percent, from 15,310 to

11,861 adults (Washington State Board for Community and Technical Colleges, 1998).

This decrease is partly explained by the strong U.S. economy, in which many potential students are attracted to the wide availability of employment opportunities. Furthermore, a national drop of 30 percent in the welfare caseload between 1993 and 1998 also reduced the pool of welfare recipients receiving education. However, policy analysts contend that PRWORA's focus on a work-first approach has played an important role in reducing community colleges' welfare population (Allen, 1998). As Finney (1998) notes, among the most common reasons for dropping out of school are welfare recipients' fear of time limits on program completion and caseworkers' advice to leave school in order to start working.

According to the 1998 AACC survey, 21 percent of responding institutions experienced a decline in their welfare-to-work program enrollment since 1996. However, the proportion of colleges reporting an increase was considerably higher, at 42.3 percent. The remaining schools indicated no change in welfare enrollment (Kienzl, 1999). The survey did not allow for conclusions to be drawn as to the reasons driving enrollment changes. However, Kienzl concludes that because "a majority of the established welfare-to-work programs are located in urban areas that, over the past few years, have seen collegewide enrollment declines anyway" (p. 5), decreases in welfare enrollments may be just as attributable to an overall downturn in enrollment as to the consequences of welfare reform. Overall, 53.8 percent of the community colleges in the survey reported offering a welfare-to-work program, with an average of 2.5 percent of their students participating in those programs. Due to respect for student confidentiality and the absence of state reporting requirements, welfare enrollment figures may be underestimates.

The Welfare Student Population in California. Perhaps the most detailed study of welfare recipients enrolled in public two-year institutions within one state was released by the California community colleges (McIntyre and Chan, 1997). According to the report, four out of five community college welfare recipients in California are female, and their average age is twenty-eight. Compared to other community college students in the state, students on welfare are only slightly more often immigrants or refugees, and 4 percent of these students identified with learning or other disabilities (compared to 3 percent of other California community college students). Welfare recipients at California community colleges are also more frequently first-time students, and fewer of them hold a high school diploma or college degree.

State Initiatives

Due to the high level of flexibility afforded to states by federal welfare legislation in constructing definitions of work activities, the role of two-year colleges in providing training for welfare recipients varies from state to state. In a review of state welfare programs, Grubb, Badway, Bell, and Castellano

(1999) point out that states with the strongest community college systems that are firmly involved in economic and workforce preparation have placed efforts in accommodating education and training in their programs for welfare recipients. "In contrast, the states with little role for community colleges in welfare and those that have paid little attention to workforce development systems, have relatively weak community colleges, or are devoted to 'work first'" (p. 32).

The variation among states in the ways they handle the education component of their welfare programs is reflected in the findings of a 1997 study by the Center for Law and Social Policy and the Center on Budget and Policy Priorities (Finney, 1998). The results of the study indicated that eleven states provided no support for postsecondary education and did not embrace it as a stand-alone work activity. Fourteen other states did not accept postsecondary education as a stand-alone activity, although a variety of support services, such as child care and transportation, were provided to welfare recipients during their education or work activities. Twenty-four states allowed their welfare recipients to finish courses they had begun prior to the implementation of welfare waivers and state plans or to begin postsecondary education, making it possible for their clients to enroll in education programs without required work activities. Following is the description of community college involvement in welfare programs adopted in three states.

Wyoming. Postsecondary education plays an important role in the state welfare plan, defining full-time education as a work activity. The state's seven community colleges, its four-year university (the University of Wyoming), and several other four-year colleges are involved in these educational activities, which are supported by state funds. With the aim of facilitating the completion of education programs by welfare recipients, the program requires students on welfare who are pursuing education to attend college full time, enroll in at least twelve credit hours, and maintain a minimum 2.0 grade point average. In order to be eligible for this program, welfare recipients must have a specified amount of work experience before enrolling at a college and are also required to work during the summer. In part because of Wyoming's small caseload, the state is able to offer highly personalized programs, and local case managers can devote individualized attention to each welfare recipient (Carnevale and Reich, 2000).

Maryland. Adopting a program combining work and education, Maryland relies on an individualized approach to education under welfare reform. This approach involves a careful assessment of welfare recipients' skills, abilities, strengths, and deficiencies to develop a plan that may include education at a community college or four-year institution. In general, a welfare recipient who had already started a vocational education program is allowed to obtain a degree before embarking on the job search process. Those without a high school diploma are encouraged to obtain general educational development (GED). Many community colleges and local departments of social services collaborate to develop specialized vocational programs to make education a more available option for welfare recipients. Furthermore, several community colleges in Maryland combine education and work by providing opportunities for community service as well as internship and work-study programs (Maryland State Department of Human Resources, 1999).

Oregon. Community colleges play a crucial role in the Oregon welfare-to-work process. The colleges are not only engaged in providing education for welfare recipients, but college representatives also act as career placement specialists at welfare offices. Their task is to participate in the state-required forty-five-day work search process and determine whether welfare customers would benefit from education and training right away—usually in case of very low levels of literacy demonstrated by welfare recipients. Welfare recipients who were not successful at finding work during the job search period participate in additional testing and career counseling at Mount Hood Community College or Portland Community College to better determine what specific skills they require. Job search development specialists, alcohol and drug specialists, job retention specialists, and teenage parenting specialists are also employed at the colleges, where welfare customers take classes and attend job search workshops. Classes and workshops comply with Oregon's work requirements without students' engagement in part-time employment. With a strong emphasis on employment, the colleges offer short-term training programs, averaging six- or eight-week sessions. In order to meet the needs of those who are not ready for employment and training programs, GED and English as a Second Language (ESL) courses are also offered. Mount Hood Community College and Portland Community College have also embarked on programs emphasizing career advancement by offering tuition waivers to those obtaining their GED, enabling them to take sixteen units of postsecondary education free of charge. In addition, the colleges collaborate with the welfare agency to provide career improvement courses, such as computer training, that current and former welfare recipients are encouraged to attend (Carnevale and Reich, 2000).

National Community College Trends

The AACC survey (Kienzl, 1999) identified activities offered at responding community colleges: on-the-job training (17.1 percent), academic instruction (36.7 percent), job-specific instruction (30.4 percent), job readiness instruction (43.5 percent), job placement assistance (30.9 percent), and other programs (10.8 percent). In addition, 54.5 percent of the colleges indicated that they provided support services in one-stop career centers, designed to create important linkages among community college students or employees and local businesses. Of colleges with one-stop career centers, 93.7 percent offered job placement services, 60.8 percent provided child care services, and 46.6 percent offered transportation assistance to their students on welfare.

Short-Term Programs. The 1998 AACC study found that the average duration of a community college welfare-to-work program is between four and eight months, well below the twelve-month time limit imposed by federal welfare legislation on vocational education to be counted as allowable work activity (Kienzl, 1999). One strategy many community colleges have adopted to meet the twelve-month requirement is the use of noncredit courses. According to Kienzl, these courses are "highly responsive to local labor market demands, and [allow] sufficient flexibility to fit the constrained schedules of welfare recipients" (p. 7). Survey responses indicated that 44 percent of courses taken by welfare-to-work participants at community colleges were noncredit, and 56 percent were for credit.

The obstacles to education and training presented by the 1996 welfare legislation (PRWORA) have received considerable criticism from educators. Grubb, Badway, Bell, and Castellano (1999) point to the existence of four- to twelve-week training programs at many community colleges and assert that the limited time frame of these programs does not meet the needs of a student population characterized by low levels of academic and occupational skills. Some short-term programs are limited to offering job search assistance, while others focus on entry-level job skills or remediation or instruction in soft skills. Furthermore, by attending noncredit courses, welfare students are discouraged from pursuing postsecondary education in long-term programs.

Quick-Employment, Skill-Building, and Mixed Strategy Programs. Quick-employment programs have traditionally concentrated on individual and group job search. In contrast, programs stressing skills development offer basic education to welfare recipients. Drawing on findings from the National Evaluation of Welfare-to-Work Strategies, Strawn (1998) concludes:

> The most successful programs are in the middle of the job search to basic education continuum, with mixed strategies of employment and skill-building services. . . . Rather than seeing employment and building skills as competing goals, the research suggests that policymakers should use a wide variety of employment, training, and other services available in support of a clear employment goal, and allow local flexibility in deciding which services are most appropriate for which people [paragraphs 7–8].

Such programs provide individualized attention to welfare recipients, concentrate on employment, involve relationships with local employers, and expect high commitment to program participation from welfare recipients. While attaining employment remains the main focus of these initiatives, basic education and skill development also receive considerable attention.

Trends in Literacy Training and Basic Education. Community colleges have traditionally been engaged in providing basic education, especially in the form of adult basic education, GED programs, and ESL and basic vocational training. However, with a primary focus on raising general literacy levels generally measured in grade-level terms and emphasizing completion of the GED, graduates of these programs have not demonstrated great gains in earnings (Jenkins and Fitzgerald, 1998). Increasingly, however, community colleges are creating the explicit connection between adult literacy programs and vocational training and are extending their offerings to programs in vocational adult basic education and vocational English as a Second Language. Although these programs have not been designed with an exclusive focus on the welfare population, they have been adopted by community colleges with the purpose of serving welfare recipients. Strawn (1998), in her review of welfare reform research, also points to the need to maintain adult basic education as part of the education plan for the welfare student population and calls for its combination with vocational training and work.

In Pennsylvania, Northampton Community College has been especially active in implementing adult literacy programs tailored to the work environment for welfare recipients (Manzo, 1997). This initiative relies on research findings suggesting higher levels of welfare independence and increased earning potential for persons possessing basic skills. A document created by the college to assist adult literacy providers in designing programs that are in accordance with welfare reform outlines two sample syllabi focusing on skills and literacy competencies necessary to perform front-office responsibilities in a medical office. The first of the two classes advances students' reading, writing, and math skills. The second course uses hands-on experience in training students to perform basic computer skills. Both courses stress the development of job search skills and positive work attitudes.

Community College Initiatives

A number of individual community colleges have developed innovative practices in response to welfare reform. Following is an outline of education and training programs at two colleges relying mainly on short-term training and offering a variety of the services described in the previous sections.

Daytona Beach Community College, Florida. The Daytona Beach Community College welfare program combines vocational training, adult basic education, and work experience in ten- to sixteen-week offerings. The program's training component is based on materials used in the beginning stages of existing certificate programs in fields ranging from nursing to modern office technology. In compliance with Florida's requirement of concurrent work and educational involvement, welfare recipients engage in work activities in their chosen fields. Adult basic education combined with vocational training is an important feature of the program. After completing the short-term programs and finding employment, graduates are encouraged to return to finish their certificates they had begun training for as part of the welfare program (Cohen, 1998).

Corning Community College, New York. The Learn to Earn Program at Corning Community College began in July 1997 in response to welfare reform. The program offers a combination of workforce development activities emphasizing the acquisition of a variety of skills sought by employers. Some of the program's features include individual literacy and basic skills assessment, the development of an individualized employment plan, short-term training focusing on the development of entry-level employment skills, volunteer and work experience opportunities, training and assistance with employment placement and maintenance, six-month postemployment support and enhanced training opportunities, and referrals to community resources to meet individual needs (Ballinger, 1998).

Recommendations for Effective Programs. Drawing on past experiences and research in job training programs, demonstration programs, and community colleges, Grubb, Badway, Bell, and Castellano (1999) provide five distinct precepts of effective welfare-to-work programs. First, an understanding of the labor market is incorporated, targeting jobs with higher earnings, strong employment growth, and opportunities for advancement. Second, academic (or remedial) education, occupational skills, and work-based learning are offered in a combination that is suitable for the targeted occupation, and due attention is paid to the training of instructors. Third, support services, such as retention programs, placement services, and case management, are provided to welfare students. Fourth, postemployment education and training opportunities are emphasized, enabling students to continue their education later. And finally, information collected on outcomes, possibly through performance measures required by federal legislation, is used to inform and improve future practices.

Conclusion

States and community colleges have developed a number of initiatives in response to PRWORA. Due to the relative novelty of these programs and practices, institutions and states will benefit from research in areas such as students' views and experiences and economic, occupational, and educational outcomes related to the limitations placed on education and training under the legislation. Furthermore, a thorough examination of exemplary programs can make all community colleges, including those not currently involved in providing education for the welfare student population, more aware of the ways and methods that maximize community colleges' long-standing commitment to furthering educational opportunities for the disadvantaged.

Note

[1]Most ERIC documents (publications with ED number) can be viewed on microfiche at over nine hundred libraries worldwide. In addition, most may be ordered on microfiche or on paper from the ERIC Document Reproduction Service (EDRS) by calling (800)443-ERIC. Journal articles are not available from EDRS but can be acquired through regular library

channels or purchased from one of the following article reproduction services: Carl Uncover: /www.carl.org/uncover/], uncover@carl.org, (800)787–7979; UMI: orders@infostore.com, (800)248–0360; or IDI: tga@isinet.com, (800)523–1850.

References

Allen, M. *Welfare Reform: Creating Opportunities or Increasing Obstacles?* Denver, Colo.: Education Commission of the States, 1998. (ED 439 772)

Ballinger, J. "Corning Community College Learn to Earn Program." Paper presented at the Responding to Welfare Reform conference, Syracuse, N.Y., Feb. 1998. (ED 425 761)

Barton, P. E., and Jenkins, L. *Literacy and Dependency: The Literacy Skills of Welfare Recipients in the United States: Policy Information Report.* Princeton, N.J.: Educational Testing Service, 1995. (ED 385 775)

Carnevale, A. P., and Reich, K. *A Piece of the Puzzle: How States Can Use Education to Make Work Pay for Welfare Recipients.* Princeton, N.J.: Educational Testing Service, 2000. (ED 441 897)

Cohen, M. *Post-Secondary Education Under Welfare Reform.* Washington, D.C.: Welfare Information Network, 1998. (ED 420 748)

Finney, J. *Welfare Reform and Postsecondary Education: Research and Policy Update.* Washington, D.C.: Institute for Women's Policy Research, 1998. (ED 445 134)

Grubb, W. N., Badway, N., Bell, D., and Castellano, M. "Community Colleges and Welfare Reform." *Community College Journal,* 1999, *69,* 30–36.

Hayes, E. "Policy Issues That Drive the Transformation of Adult Literacy." In L. G. Martin and J. C. Fisher (eds.), *The Welfare-to-Work Challenge for Adult Literacy Educators.* New Directions for Adult and Continuing Education, no. 83. San Francisco: Jossey-Bass, 1999.

Jenkins, D., and Fitzgerald, J. *Community Colleges: Connecting the Poor to Good Jobs. Policy Paper.* Denver, Colo.: Education Commission of the States, 1998. (ED 439 773)

Kienzl, G. *Community College Involvement in Welfare-to-Work.* Washington, D.C.: American Association of Community Colleges, 1999. (ED 439 774)

Manzo, D. *The Influence of Federal and State Welfare Reform on Adult Education.* Washington, D.C.: ERIC Clearinghouse on Adult, Career, and Vocational Education, 1997. (ED 412 332)

Maryland State Department of Human Resources. *Utilization of Education by Maryland's Welfare Customers.* Baltimore: Maryland State Department of Human Resources, 1999. (ED 437 515)

McIntyre, C., and Chan, C. *Educating Welfare Recipients in California Community Colleges. Part I: Student Characteristics, Activities, and Performance.* Sacramento: California Community Colleges, Office of the Chancellor, 1997. (ED 407 980)

Schmidt, P. "States Discourage Welfare Recipients from Pursuing a Higher Education." *Chronicle of Higher Education,* Jan. 23, 1998, p. A34.

Strawn, J. "Beyond Job Search or Basic Education." *Policy and Practice of Public Human Services,* 1998, *56,* 48.

Washington State Board for Community and Technical Colleges. *Welfare Enrollments in Washington Community and Technical Colleges: Fall Quarter 1997.* Olympia: Washington State Board for Community and Technical Colleges, 1998. (ED 430 641)

KATALIN SZELÉNYI *is a doctoral student in the Graduate School of Education & Information Studies at the University of California, Los Angeles.*

INDEX

SINGLE ISSUE SALE

For a limited time save 10% on single issues! Save an additional 10% when you purchase three or more single issues. Each issue is normally $28^{00}.

Please see the next page for a complete listing of available back issues.

Mail or fax this completed form to: Jossey-Bass, A Wiley Company
989 Market Street • Fifth Floor • San Francisco CA 94103-1741

CALL OR FAX

Phone 888-378-2537 or 415-433-1740 *or Fax* 800-605-2665 or 415-433-4611 (*attn customer service*)

BE SURE TO USE PRIORITY CODE ND2 TO GUARANTEE YOUR DISCOUNT!
Please send me the following issues at $25^{20} each.

Important: please include series initials and issue number, such as CC113

1. CC _____

_____

_____

$ _____ TOTAL for single issues ($25^{20} each)

_____ LESS 10% if ordering 3 or more issues

_____

$ _____ TOTAL (Add appropriate sales tax for your state. Canadian residents add GST)

❑ Payment enclosed (U.S. check or money order only)

❑ VISA, MC, AmEx Discover Card # _____ Exp. date _____

Signature _____

Day phone _____

❑ Bill me (U.S. institutional orders only. Purchase order required)

Purchase order # _____
       Federal Tax ID. 135593032   GST 89102 8052

Name _____

Address _____

_____

Phone _____ E-mail _____

For more information about Jossey-Bass, visit our website at: www.josseybass.com

OFFER EXPIRES FEBRUARY 28, 2002.   **PRIORITY CODE = ND2**

CC110 Building Successful Relationships Between Community Colleges
Clifton Truman Daniel, Hanel Henriksen Hastings
Explores current relationships between two-year colleges and the media across
the country, reviewing the history of community colleges' relationships with
members of the press, examining the media's relationships with community
college practitioners, and offering practical strategies for advancing an
institution's visibility.
ISBN: 0–7879–5427–6

CC109 Dimensions of Managing Academic Affairs in the Community College
Douglas Robillard, Jr.
Offers advice on fulfilling the CAO's academic duties, and explores the CAO's
faculty and administrative roles, discussing how to balance the sometimes
conflicting roles of faculty mentor, advocate, and disciplinarian and the
importance of establishing a synergistic working relationship with the
president.
ISBN: 0–7879–5369–5

CC108 Trends in Community College Curriculum
Gwyer Schuyler
Presents a detailed picture of the national community college curriculum, using
survey data collected in 1998 by the Center for the Study of Community
Colleges. Chapters analyze approaches to general education, vocational course
offerings, the liberal arts, multicultural education, ESL, honors programs, and
distance learning.
ISBN: 0–7879–4849–7

CC107 Gateways to Democracy: Six Urban Community College Systems
Raymond C. Bowen, Gilbert H. Muller
Features case studies of six prototypical urban community college systems,
exploring how they meet the educational and training needs of an increasingly
diverse ethnic and racial community. The studies shed light on the key issues
faced by urban community colleges, including the impact of city, state, and
federal forces on the vitality of the college; how to create an urban social
agenda with scarce resources; and how to provide equal access to all while
strengthening accountability.
ISBN: 0–7879–4848–9

CC106 Understanding the Impact of Reverse Transfer Students on Community
Colleges
Barbara K. Townsend
Presents vivid profiles of the different types of reverse transfer students—
exploring their reasons for attending, their enrollment patterns, and their
educational needs. Examines institutions' strategies for recruiting, retaining,
and serving reverse transfer students and reveals how the presence of reverse
transfer students affects policy-making.
ISBN: 0–7879–4847–0

CC105 Preparing Department Chairs for Their Leadership Roles
Rosemary Gillett-Karam
Presents the qualities that experienced department chairs cite as being crucial
to success and makes a persuasive argument for the need to develop formal
training programs for people newly appointed to these positions.
ISBN: 0–7879–4846–2

CC104 Determining the Economic Benefits of Attending Community College
Jorge R. Sanchez, Frankie Santos Laanan
Discusses various state initiatives that look at student outcomes and
institutional accountability efforts and analyses the trend to connect
accountability and outcome measures with funding.
ISBN: 0–7879–4237–5

United States Postal Service

Statement of Ownership, Management, and Circulation

1. Publication Title	2. Publication Number	3. Filing Date
New Directions for Community Colleges	0 1 9 4 _ 3 0 8 1	9/28/01

4. Issue Frequency	5. Number of Issues Published Annually	6. Annual Subscription Price
Quarterly	4	$ 66.00 _Individua $135.00 _Institutic

7. Complete Mailing Address of Known Office of Publication (Not printer) (Street, city, county, state, and ZIP+4)
989 Market St
San Francisco, CA 94103
(San Francisco County)

Contact Person
Joe Schuman
Telephone
415-782-3232

8. Complete Mailing Address of Headquarters or General Business Office of Publisher (Not printer)

Same As Above

9. Full Names and Complete Mailing Addresses of Publisher, Editor, and Managing Editor (Do not leave blank)

Publisher (Name and complete mailing address)
Jossey-Bass, A Wiley Company
(Above Address)

Editor (Name and complete mailing address) Arthur M. Cohen
Eric Clearinghouse for Community Clgs.-Univ. of Ca.
3051 Moore Hall Box 95121
Los Angeles CA 90095-1521

Managing Editor (Name and complete mailing address)

None

10. Owner (Do not leave blank. If the publication is owned by a corporation, give the name and address of the corporation immediately followed by the names and addresses of all stockholders owning or holding 1 percent or more of the total amount of stock. If not owned by a corporation, give the names and addresses of the individual owners. If owned by a partnership or other unincorporated firm, give its name and address as well as those of each individual owner. If the publication is published by a nonprofit organization, give its name and address.)

Full Name	Complete Mailing Address
John Wiley & Sons Inc.	605 Third Avenue New York, NY 10158-0012

11. Known Bondholders, Mortgagees, and Other Security Holders Owning or Holding 1 Percent or More of Total Amount of Bonds, Mortgages, or Other Securities. If none, check box ▶ ☐ None

Full Name	Complete Mailing Address
Same as Above	Same As Above

12. Tax Status (For completion by nonprofit organizations authorized to mail at nonprofit rates) (Check one)
The purpose, function, and nonprofit status of this organization and the exempt status for federal income tax purposes:
☐ Has Not Changed During Preceding 12 Months
☐ Has Changed During Preceding 12 Months (Publisher must submit explanation of change with this statement)

PS Form 3526, October 1999   (See Instructions on Reverse)

---

13. Publication Title	14. Issue Date for Circulation Data Below
New Directions for Community Colleges	Summer 2001

15. Extent and Nature of Circulation		Average No. Copies Each Issue During Preceding 12 Months	No. Copies of Single Issue Published Nearest to Filing Date
a. Total Number of Copies (Net press run)		1,772	1,800
b. Paid and/or Requested Circulation	(1) Paid/Requested Outside-County Mail Subscriptions Stated on Form 3541. (Include advertiser's proof and exchange copies)	824	823
	(2) Paid In-County Subscriptions Stated on Form 3541 (Include advertiser's proof and exchange copies)	0	0
	(3) Sales Through Dealers and Carriers, Street Vendors, Counter Sales, and Other Non-USPS Paid Distribution	0	0
	(4) Other Classes Mailed Through the USPS	0	0
c. Total Paid and/or Requested Circulation [Sum of 15b. (1), (2),(3),and (4)] ▶		824	823
d. Free Distribution by Mail (Samples, complimentary, and other free)	(1) Outside-County as Stated on Form 3541	0	0
	(2) In-County as Stated on Form 3541	0	0
	(3) Other Classes Mailed Through the USPS	1	1
e. Free Distribution Outside the Mail (Carriers or other means)		156	158
f. Total Free Distribution (Sum of 15d. and 15e.) ▶		157	159
g. Total Distribution (Sum of 15c. and 15f) ▶		981	962
h. Copies not Distributed		791	818
i. Total (Sum of 15g. and h.) ▶		1,772	1,800
j. Percent Paid and/or Requested Circulation (15c. divided by 15g. times 100)		84%	84%

16. Publication of Statement of Ownership
☒ Publication required. Will be printed in the Winter 2001 issue of this publication. ☐ Publication not required.

17. Signature and Title of Editor, Publisher, Business Manager, or Owner
Susan E. Lewis
[signature] Vice President & Publisher/Periodicals
Date 9/28/01

I certify that all information furnished on this form is true and complete. I understand that anyone who furnishes false or misleading information on this form or who omits material or information requested on the form may be subject to criminal sanctions (including fines and imprisonment) and/or civil sanctions (including civil penalties).

Instructions to Publishers

1. Complete and file one copy of this form with your postmaster annually on or before October 1. Keep a copy of the completed form for your records.

2. In cases where the stockholder or security holder is a trustee, include in items 10 and 11 the name of the person or corporation for whom the trustee is acting. Also include the names and addresses of individuals who are stockholders who own or hold 1 percent or more of the total amount of bonds, mortgages, or other securities of the publishing corporation. In item 11, if none, check the box. Use blank sheets if more space is required.

3. Be sure to furnish all circulation information called for in item 15. Free circulation must be shown in items 15d, e, and f.

4. Item 15h., Copies not Distributed, must include (1) newsstand copies originally stated on Form 3541, and returned to the publisher, (2) estimated returns from news agents, and (3), copies for office use, leftovers, spoiled, and all other copies not distributed.

5. If the publication had Periodicals authorization as a general or requester publication, this Statement of Ownership, Management, and Circulation must be published; it must be printed in any issue in October or, if the publication is not published during October, the first issue printed after October.

6. In item 16, indicate the date of the issue in which this Statement of Ownership will be published.

7. Item 17 must be signed.

Failure to file or publish a statement of ownership may lead to suspension of Periodicals authorization.

PS Form 3526, October 1999 (Reverse)